# DEATH MAKES A HOLIDAY

# DEATH MAKES A HOLIDAY

## A CULTURAL HISTORY OF HALLOWEEN

## DAVID J. SKAL

BLOOMSBURY

Published by Bloomsbury, New York and London
Distributed to the trade by Holtzbrinck Publishers
Cataloging-in-Publication Data is available from the Library of Congress

ISBN 1-58234-230-X

First U.S. Edition 2002

10 9 8 7 6 5 4 3 2

Typeset by Hewer Text Limited, Edinburgh
Printed in the United States of America by
R.R. Donnelley & Sons, Harrisonburg

*For Mom and Dad,*
*from your little monster.*

# CONTENTS

*When the owls begin to hoot,*
*Quickly don your mummer's suit,*
*Steal softly out and don't be late,*
*For Hallowe'en decides your fate!*

– an early-twentieth-century postcard

# THE CANDY MAN'S TALE

ECAUSE IT WAS raining on Halloween 1974, Ronald Clark O'Bryan, a thirty-year-old optician in suburban Houston, accompanied his eight-year-old son Timothy and five-year-old daughter Elizabeth on their eagerly awaited neighborhood rounds of trick or treat.

Cautious parents knew that Halloween was already the most dangerous night of the year for children, even without rain. Halloween was traditionally believed to be the night when the veil between life and death was at its most transparent. On a purely statistical basis, this was indeed true. Youthful traffic fatalities rose precipitously and tragically every October 31, owing to masked kids' drastically reduced fields of vision, not to mention the reduced visibility of the children themselves, often dressed in costumes that merged dangerously with the murk.

Ronald O'Bryan was just one foot soldier in a new, nationwide army of vigilant parents who took to the streets with their children each Halloween. It had once been considered safe for children to roam unchaperoned through their neighborhoods on Beggars' Night, but now parents were wary. They weren't concerned about the children's mischief historically associated with the holiday – the soaped windows, toilet-papered trees, and quaintly toppled outhouses were mostly things of the nostalgic past. Most modern children, in fact, would be totally baffled if a contrarian householder demanded a trick in lieu of dispensing the expected sweet. Now, many commentators bemoaned the transaction's degeneration into an empty consumer ritual without rhyme, reason, or reciprocity. The anthropologist Margaret Mead, observing the decline of any implied threat in "trick or treat" by the mid-1970s, waxed nostalgic about earlier times when trick-or-treating had a distinct role in the socializing of children: "It was the one night in the year when the child's world and the adult's world confronted each other and children were granted to take mild revenge on the adults."

Somehow, Halloween no longer had anything to do with extending latitude or license to children. It was more about the reaffirmation of parental control, a ceremonial reassurance of the family's integrity and stability in an uncertain world. By 1974, the bright economic promises of the post-World War II era had faded and, for many, even soured. The unsavory Watergate revelations seriously eroded the idealism of many Americans. Supporting a family, much less protecting it, had become acutely difficult for countless young breadwinners. Inflation had reached the worst levels in twenty-seven years, and unemployment was skyrocketing. Gas lines were everywhere. Halloween handouts were just about the only relief available to the working wounded.

Ronald O'Bryan himself was in considerable debt, even threatened with the repossession of his car. Financial problems had already forced him to give up home ownership. But if these things were on his mind October 31, 1974, he didn't share them with his children. O'Bryan's only Halloween mask was a happy face – his own.

This day was about the kids. Ronald O'Bryan would see to it.

The O'Bryan children eschewed the traditional, homemade guises of mischief-making witches, ghosts, and goblins, and instead wore officially licensed, profit-making costumes inspired by the

1968 motion picture *Planet of the Apes* and its successful franchise of sequels. Corporate authorization and control now seemed to be just as much a part of the new Halloween as the exercise of parental prerogatives.

A few years earlier, America's master fantasist Ray Bradbury published *The Halloween Tree*, a nostalgic and parent-free paean to the Halloween of his own midwestern childhood, in which the holiday had nothing to do with movie merchandising, but rather with a profound childhood initiation into the mysteries of existence and nonexistence: "*Night and day. Summer and winter, boys. Seedtime and harvest. Life and death. That's what Halloween is, all rolled up in one. Noon and midnight. Being born, boys. Rolling over, playing dead . . .*"

Of course, almost no one harvested their own crops any more.

But still, sometimes, people harvested each other.


By 1974, traditional Halloween bogeymen were decidedly on the wane. As adults reclaimed and reshaped the holiday in their own shadow image, new kinds of hobgoblins were on the prowl. Befitting the tumultuous politics of the time, one of the most popular Halloween masks of 1974 was not a traditional gargoyle, but that of the disgraced United States president, Richard Nixon, a political effigy tossed on the Halloween bonfire of public ridicule.

The social strife rising from the Vietnam War had made it clear that there was no longer a consensus about root American values. Cynicism was creeping everywhere. Ever since the assassination of President Kennedy, a gnawing sense that the United States was somehow a "sick society" had taken hold in the popular imagination; the phrase had become a virtual mantra of cultural commentary. The postwar suburban sprawl that created a vast new landscape for trick-or-treating also fostered a new kind of anonymity and anomie. If there were crimes in the White House, what about the house next door? The pressure for two-income households resulted in less time for families to spend meaningful time together, and fostered fear that developmental harm was being done to children. Pornography was suddenly tolerated, if not celebrated. Drug use was rife, and rising. The whole natural world, environmentalists claimed, was being slowly poisoned. Rachel Carson's best-seller *Silent Spring* calmly informed readers about omnipresent "elixirs of death." "For the first time in the history of the world," Carson wrote, "every human being is now subjected to contact with dangerous chemicals, from the moment of conception until death." In short, any number of things were perceived as threats to the family, and to children in particular.

It was, therefore, not surprising that this period saw a peculiar but persistent urban legend begin to congeal. There were monsters among us, it was believed – ordinary-looking but supremely malevolent trickster-terrorists who deliberately poisoned or booby-trapped children's Halloween candy. The Halloween terrorist was faceless and fathomless, the archetypal Other, evil incarnate.

Young children weren't being poisoned domestically, but a certain unsweetened jelly called napalm had recently rained down on the Vietnamese counterparts of American grade-schoolers, and we saw the pictures. Untold numbers of postadolescents were dying in booby-trapped rice paddies. The younger generation was indeed at risk, and there were images that seemed to prove it wherever one looked.

The wildly popular 1973 film *The Exorcist* begins with innocent Halloween imagery, escalating into a surreal Götterdämmerung of a young girl poisoned not by Halloween candy but by a deliciously effective stand-in: the devil himself. At the height of the Vietnam conflict, American parents were already anxious about their children and the frightening substances and ideas which might threaten them materially or pollute them politically.

*The Exorcist* conveyed a simple, potent message: Evil is real. And it will do just about anything to get at your children.

Since demonic possession was never much of a real issue in mainstream American life, the extraordinary success of *The Exorcist* might be best explained as a veiled self-recognition by the public in a time when many families were indeed being torn apart, if not by psychokinesis and the corrosive effects of green vomit, then by political acting-out and violent disagreements with children over the war, politics, and culture. To many parents, Linda Blair's spook-house persona may have been hardly distinguishable, at least on a gut level, from the matted-haired, obscenity-spouting war protesters and hippies who were taking up an increasingly disturbing amount of cultural time in the early 1970s. Like Linda Blair's levitating Regan, they seemed to operate on a different moral plane entirely – just like the insidious, invidious, elusive-but-omnipresent Halloween-candy tamperer.

It was during this tumultuous period that the *New York Times* gave its distinguished imprimatur to the Halloween terrorist legend:

Those Halloween goodies that children collect this weekend on their rounds of "trick or treating" may bring them more horror than happiness. Take for example that plump red apple that Junior gets from a kindly old woman down the block. It may have a razor blade hidden inside. The chocolate "candy" bar may be a laxative, the bubble gum may be sprinkled with lye, the popcorn balls may be coated with camphor, the candy may turn out to be packets containing sleeping pills.

The *Times* reflected the sociopolitical overtones of the legend in quoting Dr. Reginald Steen, a Hempstead, Long Island, psychiatrist who had strong, right-leaning ideas about the possible cause of sadistic Halloween incidents. It was "the permissiveness in today's society" that was responsible. "[P]eople who give harmful treats to children see criminals and students in campus riots getting away with things . . . they think they can get away with it, too."

Within a few years of the *New York Times*'s authoritative warning piece, newspapers everywhere routinely warned parents to guard against Halloween sadists, giving the danger equal footing with more sensible concerns about flammable costumes. There was, however, one problem with the media's uncritical acceptance of the reportings: a report is a very different thing from a confirmed tampering, much less an actual injury or death. In keeping with the spirit of Halloween, hoaxes were afoot, too – lots of hoaxes, as it turned out.

Most of the reports involved only the alleged discovery of pins, needles, and razor blades in treats, with no follow-ups or arrests, much less physical harm done to anyone. Joel Best and Gerald T. Horiuchi, researchers at California State University, concluded, "Children who go trick-or-treating know about Halloween sadism; they have been warned by their parents, teachers and friends. A child who 'discovers' an adulterated treat stands to be rewarded with the concerned attention of parents, and, perhaps, police officers and reporters." Similarly, parents who claim to have discovered hidden dangers receive positive attention from peers and public authorities.

Actual cases involving minor injuries do occasionally occur, but they are so rare and scattered that they do not constitute a significant pattern. Best and Horiuchi examined seventy-six cases of Halloween sadism reported by the *New York Times*, the *Los Angeles Times*, the *Chicago Tribune*, and the *Fresno Bee* between 1958 and 1984. They found "no reports where an anonymous sadist caused death or a life-threatening injury," and that "there is no justification for the claim that Halloween sadism stands as a major threat to U.S. children." A decade earlier, *Editor and Publisher* had reached the same conclusion.

Rather than warning the public against legitimate threats, the accumulation of such reports may have succeeded mostly in giving people ideas. Take, for example, the case of the Detroit five-year-old Kevin Toston, who died of a heroin overdose, attributed by his family to adulterated Halloween candy. More people, no doubt, read the initial report than the subsequent accounts, in which it was revealed that the boy's family had contrived the evidence of poisoning to divert attention from a drug-dealing relative. The boy had inadvertently consumed a fatal dose of his uncle's stash.

If nothing else, urban legends managed to restore the element of death anxiety to a Halloween mystique that had been pretty much stripped of its primal resonance. It was not, perhaps, quite as gratifying as the delicious metaphysical chill earlier generations derived from Halloween ghost stories, fortune-telling, and the occasional midnight-dare foray into a deserted cemetery.

By October 1974, there was still no substantiated account of a single Halloween-candy poisoning.

But Ronald O'Bryan had heard all the stories, and he knew that everybody else had heard them, too.

The O'Bryans weren't alone on their soggy Halloween trek. They were joined by family friend Jim Bates and his two children, Kimberly and Mark, ages eleven and eight respectively. The Bateses and O'Bryans had been neighbors until just recently. Because of mounting debts, the O'Bryans had sold their Pasadena home and moved into an apartment in the nearby but less desirable area of Deer Park. Halloween was a reunion of sorts for the kids and the parents. The families, including Ronald's wife, Dayenne, had gathered for an early-evening dinner to precede the trick-or-treat ritual. Mrs. Bates prepared a nice pork roast.

Although Ronald Clark O'Bryan wore no costume that night, he had managed to change his own stripes as a breadwinner rather frequently, holding no less than twenty-one jobs in the previous ten years. People who knew him later would recall that he had grandiose ambitions of transforming himself into "Mr. Big" through implausible get-rich-quick schemes.

Like Halloween itself, the name O'Bryan is rooted in the ancient, tumultuous history of England and Ireland. The holiday crossed the Atlantic with the great wave of Irish emigration that followed the devastating potato famine of the late 1840s. Like a medieval plague, the crop blight, starvation, and epidemics that followed decimated the Irish population and economy and drove nearly two million citizens to North America. The survivors of the "coffin ships" – so called because of their appalling rates of disease and mortality – had every reason to keep alive a celebration that paid homage to death, or at least contained and tamed its memory in a controllable ritual. The emigrants knew full well how thin the boundary between life and nonlife could be.

In the Irish tradition, the spirits of Halloween included much more than the souls of the departed. There were also fairy-beings and witches – not to mention the devil himself. As an 1896 seasonal ditty in *Harper's Weekly* put it,

> *Pixie, kobold,[1] elf, and sprite*
> *All are on their rounds to-night, –*
> *In the wan moon's silver ray*
> *Thrives their helter-skelter play.*

"Helter-skelter" referred to the chaotic pranks of the fairy-folk, who were said to steal babies, "leaving in their place changelings,

1. A gnomelike creature of German folklore.

goblins who were old in wickedness while still in the cradle, possessing superhuman cunning," wrote Halloween historian Ruth Edna Kelley. Costumed children, of course, were a species of symbolic changelings. "One way of getting rid of these demon children was to ill-treat them so that their people would come back for them, bringing the right ones back." Ambivalence about children and childhood was always a special component of Halloween. Costumes let children express their antisocial selves, and also gave adults permission to view them literally as less-then-idealized beings.

Perhaps the most famous popular-culture evocation of children indulging their wildest Halloween fantasies about a murderous war between the young and the old can be found in Vincente Minnelli's classic MGM musical *Meet Me in St. Louis*. The film was released in 1944 – coincidentally the year of Ronald O'Bryan's birth – but, in a delightfully unforgettable sequence, depicts Halloween as practiced in 1903 Missouri. Mild forms of mock mayhem are encouraged by the adults, and the children wildly fantasize about torture and murder. Eight-year-old Tootie Smith (played by Margaret O'Brien) accepts a dare to throw flour in the face of a hated neighbor, whom she believes poisons hapless cats and incinerates them in his furnace at midnight. Needless to say, she scares herself far more than the householder. Nonetheless, she runs breathlessly back to the other children to recount her own rapturous apotheosis of the encounter: "I killed him!"

On Halloween it was possible to have whatever outrageous thing you wanted. Roles and fortunes could be reversed, imbalances balanced, scores settled. Like Margaret O'Brien's Tootie, you could even fantasize about homicide.

As another Margaret (this one named Mead), noted, "Long ago in medieval Europe, there was a folk belief that Halloween was the one occasion when people could safely evoke the help of the devil in some enterprise."

And, whatever transpired, you could always blame it on the bogeyman.

The rain had increased and Elizabeth O'Bryan had already had enough and retreated to the Bateses' house. When the remaining children returned empty-handed from one darkened home, Ronald O'Bryan went back himself to try. A rain slicker was his only costume, a flashlight his only jack-o'-lantern. He caught up with the main group a short time later, congratulating Bates on having such "rich" neighbors. "Look what they're giving out." He was holding five Giant Pixy Stix, a popular confection consisting of a long straw filled with sweet-sour sugar granules. The product was named, no doubt, to evoke the magic and wonder of the fairy-folk, entirely dispensing with the element of menace.

Back at the Bateses' house, O'Bryan gave four of the candies to the children. Then another soggy quartet of trick-or-treaters showed up at the door. O'Bryan distributed pieces of gum to the group at the door, then displayed the magic wand of the fifth Pixy Stix. The children were thrilled at the prospect of such a special treat. O'Bryan asked who wanted it. Ten-year-old Whitney Parker recognized O'Bryan as a congregant at his church, and told him so.

He was rewarded with the fifth Pixy Stix.

The Bateses and the O'Bryans said their Halloween good-byes and Ronald, Dayenne, Timothy, and Elizabeth returned to their apartment. Timothy begged for a single treat before bedtime – the prize of the evening's take, the Giant Pixy Stix. Elizabeth didn't want any. Timothy apparently didn't notice, or care, that the end of the straw had been opened, then stapled back together. When the contents proved to be too clumpy to trickle out of the straw properly, O'Bryan rolled the wand between his fingers to break down the contents so his son could better enjoy them. Timothy complained that it tasted bitter, so his father went to the kitchen and fetched him some sweet Kool-Aid to wash it down.

According to his father, about thirty seconds after he had left the room, Timothy cried out, "Daddy, Daddy, my stomach hurts!" O'Bryan then related finding his son in the bathroom, "convulsing, vomiting, and grasping" before going suddenly limp.

For Timothy O'Bryan, the thin Halloween veil between life and death dissolved entirely and utterly. The boy was dead before he reached the hospital. The cause was straightforward but nonetheless shocking: Timothy had ingested enough potassium cyanide to kill three adults. Cyanide has many legitimate industrial uses, but as a poison it acts swiftly as a chemical asphyxiant, blocking the ability of oxygen to bond with hemoglobin. Victims sometimes experience the taste of bitter almonds before their death throes begin; their air-starved blood often takes on the appearance of chocolate syrup. Timothy was pronounced dead at Southmore Hospital at ten-thirty P.M., ninety minutes after ingesting his treat.

By eleven P.M. the police had arrived at the Bateses' house. Remarkably, neither of the Bates children had eaten the candy; their mother didn't want them to mess up the house with powdered sugar. Mr. Bates admitted, however, that he had been tempted to eat one of the treats himself. Whitney Parker had started to open the candy, but he was stopped by his parents, who told him to wait until the following day. He fell asleep with the poison lying near his head until two A.M., when the police rang the doorbell.

The following morning, O'Bryan retraced the trick-or-treat route with the police, but was unable to identify the source of the poisoned candy. He spoke to the press, describing Timothy as having been "all boy. He loved football, basketball, anything. He never met a stranger. But I have my peace knowing Tim is in heaven now."

The same morning, without press or police present, he called the insurance agent who, nine days before, had executed two new twenty-thousand-dollar insurance policies on Timothy and Elizabeth to supplement their existing ten-thousand-dollar policies. O'Bryan had forged his wife's signature as cobeneficiary. Now O'Bryan wanted to know exactly what he had to do to collect.

At the funeral the next day, O'Bryan brought tears to the congregation when he sang a personalized version of the traditional hymn "Blessed Assurance":

> Blessed assurance, Jesus is Tim's!
> O what a foretaste of glory divine!
> Heir of salvation, purchase of God,
> Born of His Spirit, washed in His blood.
>
> This is Tim's story, this is Tim's song,
> Praising his Savior, all the day long;
> This is Tim's story, this is Tim's song,
> Praising his Savior, all the day long.

Jim Bates, however, was more disturbed than moved at the service. He arrived to serve as a pallbearer but, upon entering the chapel, was stunned that O'Bryan was so oblivious to the presence of his son's coffin that he literally walked straight into it. "At that point," he told a reporter, "I knew something was wrong."

The insurance agent also suspected something irregular, and called the police on his own. Meanwhile, the investigators took O'Bryan on a second, postfuneral tour of the Halloween route. He now recollected the image of a hairy arm offering the poisoned treats, but could recover no other memories that would help identify the culpable party.

Others did remember things, however. Like the three people he had openly engaged in conversation about the toxicity and availability of potassium cyanide in the month before Halloween. His specific interest in confirming the lethal dose. His desire to purchase the poison at the lowest price possible. His refusal to consider any insurance policy on his children except one that would provide a full payout immediately after the payment of a single, $106 quarterly premium.

The day after Timothy's funeral, Ronald Clark O'Bryan was arrested and charged with the murder of his only son and the attempted murder of his daughter and three other children. He pleaded his innocence, offering no refutation of the overwhelming body of evidence against him. He went to trial in late May of the following year for his son's killing, and on June 3, 1975, the jury deliberated only forty-five minutes before convicting him. The next day, the same panel required only seventy minutes to sentence him to death by electrocution.

O'Bryan's attorneys immediately filed a motion for a new trial on procedural grounds, not on any exculpatory evidence. The motion was denied, triggering nine contentious years of appeals and stays.

In the meantime, the media revisited the case each subsequent Halloween season, and the legend grew. The fact that the crime was a calculated crime for profit, not a random menace, did nothing to stop the Halloween sadist myth.

John Carpenter's film *Halloween*, released in 1978, played to the public's ready receptivity to the idea of a faceless Halloween murderer, and made a fortune. The film inspired a host of popular sequels; one of them, *Halloween III: Season of the Witch* (1983), dropped the slasher story line of the rest of the series and instead presented a stand-alone dark fantasy of a mad inventor who contaminates children's masks with supernaturally charged slivers from Stonehenge.

The late 1970s also saw the monstrous crimes of Chicago serial murderer John Wayne Gacy (a.k.a. Pogo, the "Killer Clown").

Although the killings were not specifically Halloween-related, they carried a sickly aura of Halloween masquerade nonetheless. The media macabrely juxtaposed the element of Gacy's costumed volunteer work for hospitals and charitable events with the sickening sex murders of young men. Games of deadly dress-up, it seemed, could happen anywhere, at any time.

Similarly, the baffling Atlanta child murders – thirty killings between 1979 and 1981 – added to a growing sense of a faceless, homicidal threat to the young. Three of the killings were discovered during the 1980 Halloween season, two in October and another murdered child reported missing on November 1. During the wave of terror, Atlanta's mayor and city council asked parents to cancel Halloween activities entirely. A compromise was reached, in which an organization called STOP, made up of parents of ten murdered Atlanta children, coordinated a Saturday afternoon alternative Halloween celebration with a substantial police presence. The following year Wayne Williams was convicted of two of the crimes and sentenced to consecutive life terms, but many still believe that Williams was not responsible for all the murders.

Finally, in the fall of 1982, the previously baseless fear of random poisoning became an unnerving reality. Seven people in the Chicago area died after ingesting potassium cyanide that had been crudely inserted in emptied Extra-Strength Tylenol capsules, then planted in six area stores. The first victim was a twelve-year-old girl; among the other victims, three members of a single family were wiped out. The only person ever brought to trial was an opportunist who attempted a blackmail hoax, but the actual perpetrator was never found.

Because the Tylenol murders occurred shortly before Halloween, a wave of treat-tampering anxiety spread nationwide. The *New York Post* ran a typical headline on page one: TRICK OR TERROR, with the unsubtle subtitle NATIONWIDE POISON CANDY ALERT: KEEP KIDS AT HOME.

The offer of many local hospitals to x-ray children's candy, begun in many cities during the 1970s, took on a new momentum, though some hospital officials remained skeptical about the efficacy of X rays. One Kansas hospital ultimately backed away from the idea, because "administrators thought it might give parents a false sense of security," according to the *New York Times*. Poisons and drugs, after all, couldn't be detected by X rays.

The identity and motive of the Tylenol killer may never be known, but it is not unreasonable to assume that the thoroughly ingrained urban legend of Halloween treat-tampering may have provided a powerful suggestive template for the killer.

Meanwhile, the only public face ever placed on a Halloween child murderer was that of Ronald O'Bryan, by now long media-christened as "The Candy Man." And, rather like Michael Myers, the indefatigable slasher of the *Halloween* movies, O'Bryan seemed unkillable and unstoppable. No matter how many times his execution was ordered, some kind of crazy sequel was always in the works. At one point, State District Judge Michael McSpadden ordered O'Bryan's execution (now by lethal injection, owing to a change in Texas death penalty laws) for October 31, and offered to drive the offending trickster to the death house personally. But more legal maneuvering by O'Bryan's defense attorneys prevented this bit of seasonal poetic justice.

Ronald Clark O'Bryan was put to death by lethal injection on March 30, 1984. In his final statement, he did not admit his guilt or even mention his son, except to say that "we as human beings do make mistakes and errors." He forgave all who took part in any way in his death, and asked for the forgiveness of anyone he had offended in any way during his thirty-nine years on earth.

His last meal, as recorded by the Texas Department of Criminal

Justice, consisted of a medium-to-well-done T-bone steak, french fries and ketchup, whole-kernel corn, sweet peas, a lettuce and tomato salad with egg and French dressing, iced tea with sweetener, saltines, Boston cream pie, and rolls.

He didn't ask for candy.

# ONE

# THE HALLOWEEN MACHINE

ALL IT SAMHAIN, Summer's End, All Hallows' Eve, November Eve, or Witches' Night – Halloween has its essential roots in the terrors of the primitive mind, which made no distinction between the waning of the sun and the potential extinction of the self. Ancient rituals of sacrifice and supplication were employed to guarantee a good harvest and, by extension, continued earthly existence.

In northern climates, harvest time was, or seemed, the very death of nature. As Robert Chambers, the great Victorian chronicler of holidays, characterized October: "As the fallen leaves career before us – crumbling ruins of summer's beautiful halls – we cannot help thinking of those who have perished – who have gone before us, blown forward to the grave by the icy blasts of Death."

Because life itself was literally in the balance at harvest, the close proximity of the visible world and the spirit world was more than metaphor. And so the tradition grew: for one night each year, permission would be granted to mortals to peer into the future, divine their fates, communicate with supernatural entities, and otherwise enjoy a degree of license and liberty unimaginable – or simply unattainable – the rest of the year.

The Halloween machine turns the world upside down. One's identity can be discarded with impunity. Men dress as women, and vice versa. Authority can be mocked and circumvented. And, most important, graves open and the departed return.

Of course, the "return of the dead" is an evocative allegory for the return or expression of just about anything that's been buried, repressed, or stifled by the living. What's "dead" doesn't necessarily look like a walking corpse – just take a look at the variety of secret selves on parade at any Halloween celebration today. People "resurrect" themselves, besequinned and befeathered, as glamorous movie gods and goddesses, comic-book superheroes, immortal robots, insatiable satyrs, and inflatable sex balloons. Pneumatic breasts and phalluses bounce and bob everywhere. Fantastic, towering wigs and headdresses emblematize the startling energies that lurk in the minds beneath.

But attending these lively carnival images – always – are the classic images of mortality and the grave: skeletons, vampires, zombies, and ghosts. The grand marshal of the Halloween parade is, and always has been, Death.

At Halloween, the living often make themselves appear dead, but this is only one night of the calendar. Down at the local mortuary for the rest of the year, extraordinary measures are taken to make the dead seem alive. As commentators ranging from Elisabeth Kübler-Ross to Jessica Mitford have reminded us, American culture has considerable difficulty looking death in the eye. Modern embalming practices as cataloged by Mitford indeed amount to a macabre and evasive masquerade. In *The American Way of Death*, Mitford describes the evolution of modern funeral rituals into a "grotesque cloud-cuckoo-land where the trappings of Gracious Living are transformed, as in a nightmare, into the trappings of Gracious Dying."

Like death, Halloween is also subject to decorative, euphemistic rites. The unruly energies and overtly morbid aspects of Halloween have always been targeted for control, from the early Christian church to present-day mavens of political correctness. Always, the goal is the same: to tame the holiday, to somehow make it "nice." And nobody makes it nicer than Martha Stewart, America's formidable and self-created doyenne of the domestic arts. As authorized by Stewart in her recent book *Halloween: Delicious Tricks and Wicked Treats for Your Scariest Halloween Ever*, the behavior modification of the holiday is complete.

For Stewart, everything about Halloween is Perfectly Under Control. It is a celebration oddly devoid of celebrants, especially children, who appear only sporadically throughout the book like well-behaved centerpieces, or, in one photo, completely hidden from view as a designer-sheet spook. Some of the decorations are decidedly child unfriendly, like the votive candles placed in cutout paper bags and arranged precariously on a staircase. But it's not the kids' fun or safety that's important. As Margaret Mead noted a quarter century ago, "It is now the mothers of very small children who get a kick out of Halloween, buying or making the costumes for them . . . while the small performers, trying to overcome shyness, hardly grasp what it is to be a witch or ghost."

On one level, the Martha Stewart mystique is ideally suited to Halloween, its veneration of inanimate objects perfectly appropriate to the holiday's pagan roots. Take pumpkins, for instance. Any whiff of death associated with the traditional jack-o'-lantern has been tastefully effaced with a skill comparable to that of the funeral-home cosmeticians so lovingly described by Jessica Mitford. Instead of scary, skull-like faces, pumpkins sport stylized, upscale designs inspired by Picasso or Matisse. Anything anthropomorphic has been transformed into pure ornament – the gourd metamorphosed into the glittering harvest equivalent of a Fabergé egg. But perhaps the ultimate toast to boomerish narcissism is Martha's monogrammed pumpkin, a pure embodiment of self-celebration with no connection whatsoever to any known form of communal holiday observance. It is time, perhaps, to establish a new one: the consumerist harvest of the ego itself.

All histories of Halloween inevitably wind back to the ancient Celtic festival of Samhain (pronounced SOW-win), which marked the death of summer and the beginning of the Celtic new year. The Celts comprised a wide range of peoples who inhabited the British Isles and parts of Northern Europe prior to the Roman invasions, and Samhain was one of their two major sun festivals (the other, Beltane, was the spring celebration of fertility). At Samhain, the veil between the natural and supernatural worlds was believed to be especially transparent. The physical portals between worlds were the *sídhe*, or fairy-mounds; many of these hillocks and barrows remain to this day, and are believed to be the sites of ancient Samhain rituals.

Modern, mass-media histories of Halloween – the kind that proliferate, sound-bite-style, every October – often leave the impression that the holiday has been handed down, more or less intact, from Celtic antiquity (similarly hollow claims are often made for the very modern religion of Wicca). In reality, contemporary Halloween is a patchwork holiday, a kind of cultural Frankenstein stitched together quite recently from a number of traditions, all fused beneath the cauldron-light of the American melting pot.

Antiquity, however, provides a handy tabula rasa for all kinds of modern projections, especially when historical records are skimpy.

Take the druids, for example.

The druids were the Celtic priest class, the repository of learning, tradition, and official ceremony. Because the druids left no written record of their practices and beliefs, they have long been the subject of fanciful speculation, alternately demonized and romanticized with the fashions of the times, and are often evoked in histories of Halloween. The druids are also linked in the popular imagination with Stonehenge and its mysteries, although the paleolithic edifice predates the Celts by a thousand years.

Julius Caesar was one of the few classical writers to record firsthand impressions of the Celts and druids, but, as the leader of an invading army eager to claim the Celtic lands for Rome, he may have been less than fair-handed in his assessments. "The whole Gaulish nation," he wrote, "is to a great degree devoted to super-stitious rites." One of their leading dogmas, according to Caesar, was "that souls are not annihilated, but pass after death from one body to another, and they hold that by this teaching men are much encouraged to valor, through disregarding the fear of death."

Death anxiety could also be circumvented by inflicting mortality on a designated vessel:

> . . . those who are afflicted with severe diseases, or who are engaged in battles and dangers, either sacrifice human beings for victims, or vow that they will immolate themselves, and these employ the Druids as ministers for such sacrifices, because they think that, unless the life of man be repaid for the life of man, the will of the immortal gods cannot be appeased. They also ordain national offerings of the same kind. Others make wicker-work images of vast size, the limbs of which they fill with living men and set on fire.

The image of the druids has shifted and reshifted through the centuries; they are alternately bloodthirsty pagans or paleo-tree-huggers, but always, somehow, infinitely wise and in perfect harmony with the cycles of the earth.

The Romans brought their own pagan mythology and celebrations to Britain, including the November 1 harvest festival of Pomona, goddess of the orchards, and the masked revels of Saturnalia, the winter solstice. Pomona's association with the apple no doubt fostered the fruit's later prominence in Halloween games and festivities (the apple link persists, however darkly, in the modern Halloween legend of the razor blade in the apple).

In his crusade to convert Ireland to Christianity in the fifth century, Saint Patrick appropriated many of the customs and symbols of the Celts, including the use of bonfires to celebrate church holy days and the superimposition of the pagan sun symbol onto the Christian cross. The legend of Patrick driving the snakes from Ireland is essentially an allegory of his ridding the country of pagans; in reality, snakes were never indigenous to Ireland.

In the ninth century, Pope Gregory IV established the Feast of All Saints on November 1, another calculated move to align traditional pagan festivals with Christian holidays. November 2 was designated All Souls' Day around 1006 (it had been previously celebrated on May 1), and thus a miniseason of observances was established, known in medieval times as Hallowtide.

According to one account, "It was customary in former times, on this day, for persons dressed in black to traverse the streets, ringing a dismal-toned bell at every corner, and calling on the inhabitants to remember the souls suffering penance in purgatory, and to join in prayer for their liberation and repose." In the words of a traditional Catholic devotional: *Lord Jesus Christ, King of glory, deliver the souls of all the faithful departed from the pains of hell, and from the depths of the pit: deliver them from the mouth of the lion, lest hell swallow them. . . . Grant that they may pass from death to life.*

In the prayer, "death" is purgatory and "life" is heaven; but on November Eve the metaphors were taken literally, in a stubborn clinging to pre-Christian customs. The souls of the dead, along with other supernatural beings, were permitted (in complete contradiction of Catholic doctrine) to vacate purgatory/hell to mingle – and munch – with mortals. Until the fifteenth century in Salerno, Italy, a practice prevailed on All Souls' Eve in which households provided "a sumptuous entertainment for the souls in purgatory who were supposed to revisit temporarily, and make merry in, the scene of their earthly pilgrimage."

> Every one quitted the habitation, and after spending the night at church, returned in the morning to find the whole feast consumed, it being deemed eminently inauspicious if a morsel of victuals remained uneaten. The thieves who made a harvest of this pious custom . . . generally took good care to avert any such evil omen from the inmates of the house by carefully carrying off whatever they were unable themselves to consume.

In Naples, All Souls' Day was the locus of a particularly macabre ritual. The charnel houses were thrown open and "lighted up with flowers, while crowds thronged through the vaults to visit the bodies of their friends and relatives, the fleshless skeletons of which were dressed up in robes and arranged in niches along the walls."

By the Renaissance, rituals of begging and charity by and for the living had joined offerings for the dead as a first-of-November ritual. In Shakespeare's *Two Gentlemen of Verona* (first performed about 1594), the lovesick Valentine is described by his clownish servant as "puling like a beggar at Hallowmas." The object of the beggar's whining was, traditionally, a "soul cake," made from oatmeal and molasses.

> *For we are all poor people,*
> *Well known to you before.*
> *So give us a cake for charity's sake,*
> *And our blessing we leave at the door.*

A great tradition of masked celebration/solicitation grew up around Guy Fawkes Day, observed throughout Great Britain and in colonial America on November 5. The day commemorated the 1605 foiling of a nefarious plot by Fawkes and others to blow up Parliament with thirty-six barrels of gunpowder, secreted in a vault beneath the legislative chambers. Fawkes was publicly hanged, then drawn and quartered for his treason, and it became popular to reenact his punishment through the festive parading of a scarecrow figure, or "Guy," outfitted with a pointed paper hat and carrying a lantern and matches. Paraders would go from door to door, begging for "a penny for the Guy," and chanting a time-honored rhyme:

> *Remember, Remember!*
> *The fifth of November,*
> *The Gunpowder treason and plot;*
> *There is no reason*
> *Why the Gunpowder treason*
> *Should ever be forgot!*

The conclusion of the celebration saw the Guy tossed onto a ceremonial bonfire, often with effigies of the pope (Fawkes was a Catholic). According to one account, the London celebration was especially "important and portentous," with the bonfire at Lincoln's Inn Fields conducted on a magnificent scale: "Two hundred cart-loads of fuel would sometimes be consumed in feeding this single fire, while upwards of thirty 'Guys' would be suspended on gibbets and committed to the flames." Over time, Guy Fawkes Day evolved more and more into a child's holiday, and by the nineteenth century illustrations of the celebration depict both the juvenile paraders and the Guy himself outfitted with masks reminiscent of the commedia dell'arte.

Hallowmas was considered the beginning of the Christmas season in England and, during the reign of Charles I in the seventeenth century, became a time for elaborate masques staged by the lawyers of London's Middle Temple. These dance recitals were major social events, and included the rich display of finery and feathers.

By the eighteenth century, elaborate masquerade had become a cultural preoccupation of English society year-round, incorporating the role reversals associated with the Roman Saturnalia and the medieval Feast of Fools, and the relaxation of social constraints associated with celebrations of May Day and Midsummer's Eve.

"Like the world of satire, the masquerade projected an anti-nature, a world upside-down, an intoxicating reversal of ordinary sexual, social and metaphysical hierarchies," writes Terry Castle in *Masquerade and Civilization*. "Its hallucinatory reversals were both a voluptuous release from ordinary cultural prescriptions and a stylized comment upon them."

These English revels certainly anticipated the spirit of modern Halloween, though the night itself was not yet associated with masking (or "guising") and, in fact, did not yet have a standard name. The word *Halloween* derives from the Middle English *hallowen* (hallowed, sacred) and the progressive contraction of *evening* to *even* to *e'en*. "All Hallows' Eve," "Hallowmas (or Hallow-Mass) Eve," "All Hallows' Fire," and "Hallow Even Fire" were some of the variations. According to the *Oxford English Dictionary*, *Halloween* first appears in print sometime during the eighteenth century in a line of dialogue from the ballad "Young Tamlane": "This night is Hallowe'en, Janet. The morn is Hallowday." Robert Burns's celebrated poem "Halloween" (1785) is both a paean to the holiday and a valuable historical document:

> *Among the bonny winding banks*
> *Where Doon rins, wimplin', clear,*
> *Where Bruce ance*[2] *ruled the martial ranks,*
> *And shook his Carrick spear,*

2. once

> *Some merry, friendly countra-folks*
>    *Together did convene,*
> *To burn their nits,[3] and pou their stocks,[4]*
>    *And haud[5] their Halloween*

Nuts, like apples, are symbols of the harvest and are obviously plentiful at the end of October. Both figure prominently in the history of Halloween. Burns's poem recorded and memorialized Halloween customs involving fortune-telling with apples and nuts as practiced in Scotland and, with certain variations, in England, Wales, Ireland, and the Isle of Man. Nuts in the Halloween fireplace represented some combination of the questioner, a sweetheart, and/ or rival suitors. In "The Spell," English poet and playwright John Gay (1685–1732) delineates the game:

> *Two hazel-nuts I threw into the flame,*
> *And to each nut I gave a sweetheart's name.*

The nut that cracked or jumped indicated fickleness or instability; by contrast, the nut that burned steadily represented undying affection. Gay describes the English custom of two nuts representing two potential sweethearts; in Burns's Scottish poem, one nut represents the questioner. In the Irish tradition, three nuts were used – the questioner flanked by a pair of love interests.

In his 1801 poem "On Nuts Burning, Allhallows Eve," Charles Graydon found a microcosm of the human experience. He describes the ritual in language unburdened by Robert Burns's thick dialect, and therefore more accessible to most modern readers:

3. nuts
4. pull their kale or cabbage stalks
5. observe, hold (a celebration)

*These glowing nuts are emblems true*
*Of what in human life we view;*
*The ill-matched couple fret and fume,*
*And thus in strife themselves consume,*
*Or from each other wildly start*
*And with a noise forever part.*
*But see the happy, happy pair*
*Of genuine love and truth sincere;*
*With mutual fondness, while they burn*
*Still to each other kindly turn:*
*And as the vital sparks decay,*
*Together gently sink away.*
*Till, life's fierce ordeal being past,*
*Their mingled ashes rest at last.*

By the eighteenth and nineteenth centuries, it is remarkable how little of Halloween's supernatural element involves spirits of the dead or other underworld entities; the fantastic component collapses into a solitary obsession: getting a sneak supernatural peek at one's future mate. Next to nuts, apples were a favorite medium for divination of a male lover. It was believed, with remarkable uniformity throughout Great Britain, that a young woman could divine her romantic future by sitting before a mirror at Halloween midnight, slicing an apple into nine pieces, and holding each piece on the tip of the knife before eating it. Upon finishing her repast, it was said, the face of her future husband would appear over her shoulder in the mirror. Just why this tradition persisted as long as it did is something of a puzzle, since no real apple-apparitions were ever convincingly documented.

The extremely popular practice of apple "bobbing" (or "ducking," or "snapping" – another name for Halloween in the north of England was "Snap-Apple Night") also had its roots in fortune-telling, though by the end of the nineteenth century it seems to have evolved into pure sport.

> Great fun goes on in watching the attempts of the youngster in the pursuit of the swimming fruit, which wriggles from side to side of the tub, and evades all attempts to capture it; whilst the disappointed aspirant is obliged to abandon the chase in favour of another whose turn has now arrived. The apples provided with stalks are generally caught first, and then comes the tug of war to win those which possess no such appendage. Some competitors will deftly *suck up* the apple, if a small one, into their mouths. Others plunge manfully overhead in pursuit of a particular apple, and having forced it to the bottom of the tub, seize it firmly with their teeth, and emerge, dripping and triumphant, with their prize. This venturous procedure is generally rewarded with a hurrah! by the lookers-on, and is recommended, by those versed in Halloween-aquatics, as the only sure method of attaining success.

A variation on the game involved snapping at a suspended apple (again, with one's hands tied behind one's back) or, more elaborately, a spinning stick with a candle on one end and an apple on the other. Vigorous dodging was required to avoid being burned by the candle or being painfully spattered with hot wax.

Other Halloween games utilizing harvest produce retained the divinatory aspect. English folklore historian William S. Walsh described a particularly durable custom: ". . . any maiden may find out at least the first letter of the name of her future husband by peeling a pippin, taking the paring by one end in her fingers, swinging it three times around her head, and then letting it drop. The pippin-paring thus dropped will surely fall in the shape of the initial of his name, as she will readily see, though the rest of the company, not having quite so discerning eyes as hers, may not."

In Scotland, young people went blindfolded into the garden to pull kale stalks; later, before the crackling fireplace, the plants would be "read" for revealing signs of the future wife or husband – short and stunted, tall and healthy, withered and old, and so on. The amount of earth clinging to the root was believed to indicate the amount of dowry or fortune the player could expect from a mate. The stalks were then hung above the door in a row, and each subsequent Halloween visitor was assigned the identity of a vegetable-spouse in turn. Cabbages and leeks were similarly used. Among other traditional fortune-telling foods was colcannon, a dish made of mashed potatoes, parsnips, and onions, in which various charms were buried. Whoever found a ring was promised marriage within the year. A thimble augured the fate of a spinster or bachelor, a key signified a trip, a coin meant wealth, and so forth.

An interesting tale of romantic Halloween divination appears in Robert Chambers's *The Book of Days* (1864), attributed to the daughter of a young couple who lived in the province of Leinster, Ireland, in the middle of the eighteenth century. On the Halloween following their daughter's birth, the mother had a compelling dream. "I thought I was dragged against my will into a strange part of the country, where I had never been before, and, after what appeared to me a long and weary journey on foot, I arrived at a comfortable-looking house. I went in longing to rest, but had no power to sit down, although there was a nice supper laid out before a good fire, and every appearance of preparations for an expected visitor." Too exhausted to stand any longer, she hurried away by the same road, then awoke and realized it had all been a dream.

Her husband listened, then sighed deeply. "My dear Sarah," he told her, "you will not long have me beside you; whoever is to be your second husband played last night some evil trick of which you have been the victim."

Some months later, the husband's health failed and Sarah was indeed left a widow as he had predicted. After a few years, her uncle, who lived some distance away, suggested that a young man of his acquaintance might find her manageable. When the young man first glimpsed her, he told the uncle in stunned amazement, "A year or two ago I tried a Halloween-spell, and sat up all night to watch the result. I declare to you most solemnly, that the figure of that lady, as I now see her, entered my room and looked at me. She stood a minute or two by the fire, and then disappeared as suddenly as she came." The young man insisted he had been wide awake, and was overcome with remorse "at having thus ventured to tamper with the powers of the unseen world." Nonetheless, he finally met the woman who had visited him in the Halloween dream. They made a good match, and were happily married.

Not all Halloween divination stories had happy endings. According to one nineteenth-century account, "several well-authenticated instances are related of persons who, either from the effects of their own imagination, or some thoughtless practical joke, sustained such severe nervous shocks, while essaying these Halloween-spells, as seriously to imperil their health."

In all likelihood, the unspecified shocks revolved around darker divination practices, not the ones concerned with living sweethearts, but rather those conjuring the demon lover, Death. On Halloween in Wales, family members would toss white stones marked with their initials into the fire, pray, and go to bed. Those who could not locate their own stone in the morning were expected to die within the year. In Ireland, "Ashes were raked smooth on the hearth at bedtime on Hallowe'en, and the next morning examined for footprints. If one was turned from the door, guests or a marriage was prophesied; if toward the door, a death." Halloween was also the time when Irish children would return to the place where they had hung up an herb called "livelong" on Midsummer Eve. Those whose herbs had retained their color would prosper, those whose plants had withered would die themselves. Scottish children replenished the population by piling up cabbage stalks before retiring on Halloween, in the belief that a new brother or sister would shortly be provided to them – this, obviously, a variation on the belief that babies were found in cabbage patches.

The vegetable symbol most associated with Halloween is, of course, the jack-o'-lantern, which also had its roots in British folklore. Jack was a perennial trickster of folktales, who offended not only God but also the devil with his many pranks and transgressions. Upon his death, he was denied entrance into both heaven and hell, though the devil grudgingly tossed him a fiery coal, which Jack caught in a hollowed turnip and which would light his night-walk on earth until Judgment Day. Jack's perpetual prank is the decoying of hapless travelers into the murky mire.

The story of Jack-o'-Lantern parallels that of Will-o'-the Wisp; both legends personify the phenomenon of fool's-fire, or ignis fatuus – the phosphorescent swamp gas long known in the bogs of Britain, and sometimes used today as a rather unconvincing explanation for UFO sightings. But just when the name became associated with the practice of carving fearsome faces into vegetables is less clear. The name certainly bears a striking similarity to Jack-o'-Lent, a puppet/scarecrow effigy of Elizabethan times which was pelted for sport on Ash Wednesday (the traditional customs of carnival had a great influence on the evolution of Halloween). The *Oxford English Dictionary* gives a date of 1663 for its first printed record of the phrase "Jack-with-the-lantern," and 1704, "Jack of lanthorns," both referring to a night watchman (which, in a sense, a jack-o'-lantern is, standing watch in windows and on doorsteps). In Sheridan's *The Rivals* (1773; act II, scene iv), the metaphorical dimension is exploited: "I have followed Cupid's jack-a-lantern, and found myself in a quagmire." Coleridge, reviewing a play in

1817, compares the characters' frisky, flitting antics to the teasing "Jack o'Lantern lights which mischievous boys . . . throw with a looking glass on the faces of their opposite neighbors."

Thus, the jack-o'-lantern is definitely associated by 1817 with spooky pranks – but not explicitly with Halloween or hollowed turnips. Although every modern chronicle of the holiday repeats the claim that vegetable lanterns were a time-honored component of Halloween celebrations in the British Isles, none gives any primary documentation. In fact, none of the major nineteenth-century chroniclers of British holidays and folk customs makes any mention whatsoever of carved lanterns in connection with Halloween. Neither do any of the standard works of the early twentieth century. Iconography seems nonexistent. The *Oxford English Dictionary* provides no clue as to when the Halloween association began; it credits the United States as the primary source of the modern definition of the jack-o'-lantern, followed by England and Ireland, but without dates or citations.

Some Halloween historians insist that the jack-o'-lantern is essentially Irish in origin; others argue for Scotland as the source of all things Halloweenish (despite Robert Burns's glaring omission of the jack-o'-lantern in his comprehensive description of Halloween toward the end of the eighteenth century).

In short, the true history of the jack-o'-lantern seems as elusive and intangible as its Will-o'-the-Wisp inspiration.

The French historian Jean Markale maintains that Irish Catholics took Halloween legends more literally than the Presbyterian Scots, who were "too puritanical to take seriously the actual presence of ancestors or relatives on the evening of Halloween" and instead popularized the jack-o'-lantern as a fanciful representation of a wandering soul.

Jack-o'-lanterns weren't the only ones to wander. One of the greatest human migrations in history was set in motion by Ireland's

catastrophic potato famine of 1846. It is inconceivable that any spare
foodstuff would be used for amusement, at Halloween or anytime,
and the lantern tradition may well have been kept alive by the Scots.
As Halloween historian Lesley Pratt Bannatyne writes, "The Irish
had precious little to pack with them in the way of wealth or
belongings, but they did manage to bring along their old-world
October 31 celebration. Wherever the Irish went – Boston, New
York, Baltimore, through the Midwest to Chicago and beyond –
Halloween followed along."

One Halloween tradition definitely exported by Ireland and
Scotland was boisterous behavior and pranking, all evidently
modeled on the fabled antics of pixies and hobgoblins. The
late-nineteenth-century historian William Shepard Walsh recorded some of the annoyances mischievous boys could concoct
from the traditional food of the holiday, cabbage. "Mischievous
boys push the pith from the stalk, fill the cavity with tow [hemp
fiber] which they set on fire, and then through the keyholes of
houses of folk who have given them offence blow darts of flame a
yard in length." The startling effect of a prank could be aural as
well as visual: "If on Halloween a farmer's or crofter's [tenant
farmer's] kail-yard still contains ungathered cabbages, the boys and
girls of the neighborhood descend upon it *en masse*, and the entire
crop is harvested in five minutes' time and thumped against the
owner's doors, which rattle as though pounded by a thunderous
tempest."

Walsh is one of the few late-nineteenth-century writers to make a
contemporary comparison between Halloween customs in America
and Britain:

In the United States it is to be regretted that the spirit of
rowdyism has in a measure superseded the kindly old customs.
In towns and villages gangs of hoodlums throng the streets,

ringing the door-bells or wrenching the handles from their sockets, and taking gates from off their hinges. In Washington the boys carry flour in a bag. Care is taken to have the web of the bags so worn that a slight blow will release a generous supply of the white powder. The bags are long and narrow, and are handled as if they were slung-shots. These the boys use upon one another as well as upon non-belligerent passers-by.

By contrast, he quotes a journalist's account of the pomp and circumstance attending a mid-Victorian Halloween celebration at Scotland's Balmoral Castle, supervised by Queen Victoria herself.

Preparations had been made days beforehand, and farmers and others for miles around were present. When darkness set in, the celebration began, and her majesty and the Princess Beatrice, each bearing a large torch, drove out in an open phaeton. A procession formed of the tenants and servants on the estate followed, all carrying huge torches lighted. They walked through the grounds and around the castle, and the scene as the procession moved onwards was very weird and striking.

The account is especially significant because it includes a rare pre-1900 description of macabre Halloween costuming. Despite modern claims, there is little primary documentation for Halloween masking, macabre or otherwise, before this time, although masquerade was richly associated with other holidays that fed the Halloween tradition – the carnival celebrations preceding Lent, the mumming and cross-dressing associated with Christmas/Saturnalia, the masked beggars of Guy Fawkes Day, and so on. The vivid particulars of Victoria's 1874 Halloween bash, however, seem to compensate for a previous dearth of detail.

. . . An immense bonfire, composed of old boxes, packing cases, and other materials, stored up during the year for the occasion, was set fire to. When the flames were at their brightest, a figure dressed as a hobgoblin appeared on the scene, drawing a car surrounded by a number of fairies carrying long spears, the car containing the effigy of a witch. A circle having been formed by the torch-bearers, the presiding elf tossed the figure of the witch into the fire, where it was speedily consumed. This cremation over, reels were begun, and were danced with a great vigor to the stirring strains of Willie Ross, her majesty's piper.

Halloween effigies crossed the Atlantic, but their precise provenance in the New World remains wobbly. An early example of a pumpkin appears as an engraving in the November 23, 1867, issue of *Harper's Weekly*, coinciding with Thanksgiving instead of Halloween. Pumpkins were indigenous to North America, though unknown in Great Britain, and, unlike turnips or beets, they were easy to hollow and carve. The first spooky use of a pumpkin in American literature appears in Washington Irving's "Legend of Sleepy Hollow" in 1819. Ichabod Crane, an annoying schoolmaster in the Dutch Hudson River settlement of Sleepy Hollow, is sent skedaddling from town by the bogus apparition of the galloping Headless Horseman, who hurls his own head at Ichabod as a final, midnight fright. The head turns out to be an ordinary pumpkin, not a jack-o'-lantern; Halloween, in fact, is never mentioned in the story at all, and was not a celebration observed by Dutch settlers in America. Modern dramatizations of the story – notably Walt Disney's 1949 animated short – inevitably, and anachronistically, superimpose Halloween on the story, if only to exploit the visual possibilities of a blazing-eyed jack-o'-lantern as the Horseman's head.

By the late 1890s, carved pumpkins were an integral part of American Halloween celebrations, judging from newspaper illustrations and commercial postcards. Still, the standard holiday chronicles of the period are oddly silent about this ubiquitous symbol of October 31. But by the turn of the century, Halloween practices and iconography were about to reach a critical mass.

Although its ancient roots are tangled in Celtic prehistory, Halloween as we know it today was ultimately created from diverse traditions that landed on American shores in the seventeenth, eighteenth, and nineteenth centuries. The Puritans had no use for the Romish rituals of Hallowtide (the dead, after all, were predestined to heaven or hell, so why pray for them?) but they believed passionately in the devil and most especially in witchcraft. Their witch-hunting zeal in New England found no real witches, but forever galvanized one of Halloween's most enduring symbols.

The Germans didn't celebrate Halloween, but they brought with them strong traditions of carnival and the supernatural. Fasnacht revels in Bavaria broke the solemnity of Lent with rowdy masked processions of skeletons, witches, and demons. Walpurgis Night, April 30, coincided with the ancient Celtic feast of Beltane, and, like Samhain, was believed to be a night when all manner of evil spirits walked the earth. (It was also the original Eve of All Souls, until the church moved the date to November.) French settlers brought memories of the medieval Feast of Fools and the Parisian Lenten carnival that gave birth to Mardi Gras. The Irish and Scots brought their fortune-telling spells, their bonfires, their fairy-worlds – but most of all, they brought the word *Halloween*.

Despite the British observations about rowdyism across the Atlantic, Halloween in Victorian America emerges from newspaper and magazine records as a genteel holiday, its energies firmly corseted to fit the fashions of the time. The emphasis is on private parties, matchmaking and fortune-telling, and games like apple-bobbing and candlestick-jumping. It is first and foremost a holiday of decorous femininity. The antisocial antics of young boys at Halloween is more the subject of humor than of real concern. A November 5, 1899, comic supplement to the *St. Louis Post-Dispatch* posits a whole menagerie of supernatural superegos that might keep young males in line: "The Bugaboos that Come after Boys Who Stay Out Nights," "The Spook that Watches All Doorbell Ringers," "The Spectre that Follows Little Boys Who Catch on Behind [ice wagons]," "The Cigarette Spook," "The Sugar Bowl Goblin," and so on.

The spirit and imagery of Halloween in America has never been so vividly documented as it was during the first decades of the twentieth century, thanks to the popular medium of picture postcards. Often elaborately printed and embossed, Halloween postcards offer a colorful and comprehensive catalog of holiday practices of the period. The earliest were the products of Raphael Tuck, a German postcard manufacturer who popularized the exchanging and collecting of exquisitely lithographed cards. Other important postcard manufacturers were the John Winsch Company, whose cards were also printed in Germany, and the Gibson Art Company of Cincinnati, best known for popularizing the "Gibson Girl" icon. The most beloved illustrator of the Halloween genre was Ellen Clapsaddle, an American painter who worked for publishers on both sides of the Atlantic and specialized in adorable depictions of cherubic youngsters; Clapsaddle's closest rival for the cuddle quotient was Frances Brundage. Although Halloween cards represented only a small percentage of the industry's total output, a century later they remain among the most prized collectibles.

Halloween postcards provide a definitive record of the importation of Gaelic holiday customs to America. A great number of the early cards feature specifically Scottish motifs (tartan plaid borders, thistles and heather, messages like "Auld Lang Syne," and the like), giving some credence to the idea that the holiday may be more Scottish than Irish. (As Halloween-collectibles authority Stuart Schneider notes, "the earliest decorations never show shamrocks, leprechauns, etc.") This, however, ignores the large overlap of customs observed by both the Irish and the Scots, and the overwhelming numbers of Irish immigrants in America at the end of the nineteenth century as opposed to Scots. Since the Irish faced particular discrimination and marginalization in America, it is possible they were simply never considered a strong market for the decidedly bourgeois imagery of picture postcards.

In terms of dominant postcard iconography, the jack-o'-lantern rules. A handful of the "Auld Lang Syne" postcards clearly depict the lost legacy of the turnip, but the vast majority feature the user-friendlier North American pumpkin. The Scottish-flavored cards frequently depict a variation on the jack-o'-lantern completely unknown today – full-figured pumpkin-people, their vegetable features not carved, instead weirdly morphed with expressive human faces, similar to the cinema's unforgettable "man in the moon" icon forged by French filmmaker Georges Méliès in 1902. These strange characters engage in all the traditional rites of human Halloween, including apple-ducking and romantic divination, as well as some truly surreal activities, like transmogrifying their round faces into hot-air Halloween balloons or weeping piteously as their hybrid visages are vivisected by knife-wielding imps or demons.

Pumpkins figure prominently in other, deliriously dreamlike imagery, transformed into fantastic carriages pulled through the night by teams of black cats, or replacing the wheels of bicycles-built-for-two pedaled through the sky by Gibson Girls, apparently in lieu of a proper broomstick. Otherwise, the jack-o'-lantern is generally presented in its traditional form as a festive euphemism for the death's-head, the triangular nose hole and rictus grin being the "dead" giveaways. All the death-related aspects of Halloween, in fact, are quarantined within the image of the Victorian/Edwardian jack-o'-lantern, whether presented alone or with a trailing ghostlike sheet attached. Skeletons, for instance, do not appear at all.

Witches are another favorite postcard motif, and it's surprising how festive they appear in print. Virtually no depictions of witches at this time appear garbed in black; the hats and habits are typically red, blue, or dark green. Witches in black raiment were largely standardized in the twentieth century by Margaret Hamilton as the Wicked Witch of the West in MGM's *The Wizard of Oz* (1939). But previously, they do not seem to have been accountable to any particular dress code.

Halloween costumes, when depicted on postcards, are not at all grotesque. Witches in particular – at least the ones imitated by mortals – are highly fashionable if not outright glamorous. Flanked by black cats and jack-o'-lanterns, beautiful women and angelic children sport conical hats, stylish frocks, and absolutely no warts. By the 1920s, the art deco aesthetic takes over, and both men and women appear in evening clothes and harlequin masks, the women's gowns stenciled with exquisite silhouettes of cats, bats, and flying witches.

Significantly, the cards also illustrate the fortune-telling practices transplanted largely intact from Scotland, Ireland, England, and Wales. Countless cards show young women performing variations on the midnight mirror-gazing ritual, as well as a divination game involving three bowls, or "luggies," one empty, one containing clear water, and the last containing foul or soapy water, or simply dirt. A blindfolded player would approach the bowls and dip his or her fingers into one. The clear water represented a virginal mate, the cloudy water or dirt represented "damaged goods," and the empty bowl the barren fate of a spinster or bachelor.

The revenant dead are notable by their absence in these super-natural parlor games, though not for lack of public interest. Séances and spiritualism were all the rage, capturing the imaginations of untold numbers of people in America and Europe year-round, and ghost stories have never been as popular as they were during the Victorian era. Advances in science and the march of materialism during the nineteenth century challenged traditional religious concepts of the afterlife, fueling an industry of mediums, table levitation, and Ouija boards. But for the time being, the original premise of Halloween – communion with the dead – was only faintly echoed in the holiday itself.

Black American folklore had many themes in common with Halloween practices imported from Europe, especially those involving charms, divination, and offerings to the dead. The admixture of African religions and Roman Catholicism known as voodoo (or vodoun) is sometimes cited as having an influence on Halloween in the South, but there are no discernible holiday motifs or practices drawn specifically from African or Caribbean folklore. Black Americans seem to have adopted and adapted old-world Halloween practices as they settled in cities where Irish and Scottish populations were already well established.

But the turn of the century did see the appearance of commercial Halloween postcards specifically depicting African Americans. Many are identical in design to their Caucasian counterparts, save for the substitution of cherubic black children, and may represent a cost-effective method to target a niche market. But most Halloween depictions of blacks are obviously intended for white audiences, and relied heavily on a blatantly negative stereotype: the superstitious "coon." As described by to historian Donald Bogle in his book *Coons, Toms, Mulattoes, Mammies and Bucks*, coons were presented as "unreliable, crazy, lazy, subhuman, good for nothing more than eating watermelons, stealing chickens, shooting craps, or butchering the English language."

Typical is a poem, "Hallowe'en Failure," by Carlyle Smith,

published in the October 29, 1910, issue of *Harper's Weekly*, hardly a publication with a significant black readership:

> *Who's dat peekin' in de do'?*
> *Set mah heart a-beatin'!*
> *Thought I see' a spook for sho*
> *On mah way to meetin'.*
> *Heerd a rustlin' all aroun',*
> *Trees all sort o' jiggled;*
> *An' along de frosty groun'*
> *Funny shadders wriggled.*

Unlike the Irish and Scots, who brought with them the central superstitions upon which Halloween is based, it was blacks who bore the brunt of condescending derision for their supposed susceptibility to scares. The stereotype would be kept alive by twentieth-century popular culture as the familiar black character whose sole purpose is to provide "comic relief" in mysteries and horror movies:

> *Who's dat by de winder-still?*
> *Gittin sort o' skeery;*
> *Feets is feelin kind o'chill,*
> *Eyes is sort o' teary.*
> *Most as nervous as a coon*
> *When de dawgs is barkin',*
> *Er a widder when some spoon*
> *Comes along a-sparkin'.*

> *Whass dat groanin' soun I hear*
> *Off dar by the gyardin?*
> *Lordy! Lordy! Lordy dear,*
> *Grant did sinner pardon!*

*I won't nebber — I declar'*
*Ef it ain't my Sammy!*
*Sambo, what yo' doin dar?*
*You can't skeer yo' mammy!*

In Elizabeth F. Guptill's "What Do You Know About Ghosts?" (1915), a farcical skit for four boys, the sole black character is "Washington Jefferson Jackson Lincoln," and he is given the full minstrel-show treatment. The other boys are proper Halloween ghosts draped in white sheets, but Washy shows up in a long black coat. The white boys tease him – doesn't he know what color ghosts are supposed to be? Washy insists his costume is appropriate. He is impersonating the ghost of his grandfather, about whom there was nothing white "cept de whites ob he eyes, an' him teef."

Washy is far more defiant and assertive than the quaking, superstitious black usually depicted in plays, films, and popular iconography of the period – often a wide-eyed pickaninny shaking in mortal fear before a sheeted specter, and perhaps with good reason. The secondary meaning of such imagery in its historical context is so blatantly transparent that it needs no interpretation at all.

For most Halloween celebrants from 1900 to 1930, the primary treat associated with Halloween was the prospect of attending a themed costume party, which were hosted for children and adults alike. Mass-market periodicals like the *Ladies' Home Journal* annually offered illustrated suggestions for the perfect festivity. Some were appealingly jejune, like the carnivalesque harvest costumes proposed by the *Journal* for Halloween 1917; others were bizarre in their stretch for sophistication, like the "Pyramids of Fun for Halloween" prescriptions at the height of the King Tut mania in 1924. Traditional Halloween symbols were re-rendered in angular, "Egyptian" fashion – the jack-o'-lantern became a glowering triangle – and

readers were encouraged to bake gingerbread mummies, to deci-
pher the hieroglyphics attending "King Jak-o-Lantern's Tomb,"
and so on.

The Dennison Manufacturing Company of Framingham, Massachusetts, was a well-established supplier of paper products when,
in 1912, it began publishing an annual series of *Bogie Books*
demonstrating how its products (crepe paper primary among them)
could be utilized in homemade Halloween costumes and decorations, as well as to market its own printed tablecloths, napkins, place
cards, and die-cut decorations. By 1925, according to collector/
historians Dan and Pauline Campanelli, "there were about ten
thousand Dennison dealers throughout the country selling Dennison products and demonstrating their uses."

The Dennison designs are classics of their kind, and many of the
company's witches, black cats, and jack-o'-lanterns survive today in
clip art collections and as rubber-stamp motifs. The original merchandise and publications are highly prized by collectors, perhaps
more for their idealized portrayal of the holiday than the holiday as it
was typically celebrated. Instead of throwing eggs or turning over
garbage cans (activities sadly on the rise following World War I),
Halloween revelers are instead invited into the kind of posh harle-
quinade that Jay Gatsby might be likely to throw at East Egg. As
rendered by Dennison's artists, the guests slouch around in forced,
art-deco poses. Pumpkin-Pierrots cavort with flappers flapping bat
wings, and everybody makes a grand entrance. "Crepe paper, in plain
colors or the gayly printed patterns, may be quickly fashioned into
charming costumes," the *Bogie Book* of 1926 informs us.

> The "slip over" is the most popular kind of costume because it
> is so simple and inexpensive to make and because it is equally
> appropriate for both boys and girls. The foundation is a straight
> strip of crepe paper cut out for the neck and hanging straight

down from front and back. To this foundation are fastened ruffles, fringe or cut-out designs. A costume of this kind is worn over a simple frock or business suit and is particularly well adapted for an informal party.

There are no depictions of flaming human torches – though the close proximity of candles and all that crepe paper suggests that such occurrences would not have been all that rare in the Roaring Twenties, when laissez-faire ruled and the Consumer Product Safety Commission didn't. And, although the *Bogie Book* assures the reader that "The costumes pictured here are easy to copy," none of them, in fact, even remotely match the facile description of the "slip over," and would clearly require considerable time and tailoring. All are the obvious work of professional designers, apparently under the influence of Erté. Nonetheless, three quarters of a century before Martha Stewart, Dennison effectively marketed the fantasy of a perfectly controlled and perfectly stylish Halloween within the reach of everyone.

What now strikes us as the time-honored rite of trick-or-treating is not referred to in any of the *Bogie Books*, and had not yet been assimilated into Halloween on a large scale. There is strong evidence that Halloween tricksters are being bought off with candy as early as 1920; packaging for Ze Jumbo Jelly Beans, manufactured in Portland, Oregon, contained the prominent message STOP HALLOWEEN PRANKSTERS.

Curiously, in the neighborhoods of New York before and after World War I a major costume and begging ritual was associated with the harvest festival of Thanksgiving, not Halloween. Betty Smith's 1943 novel *A Tree Grows in Brooklyn*[6] memorably describes

---

6. When *A Tree Grows in Brooklyn* appeared as a Broadway musical in 1951, it contained a "Halloween Ballet" meant to evoke both the children's holiday and their alcoholic father's delirium tremens. By all accounts, it was a showstopper.

this holiday as observed by poor Irish children – clearly All Hallow's Eve in everything but name.

> The street was jammed with masked and costumed children making a deafening din with their penny tin horns. Some kids were too poor to buy a penny mask. They had blackened their faces with burnt cork. Other children with more prosperous parents had store costumes: sleazy Indian suits, cowboy suits and cheesecloth Dutch maiden dresses. A few indifferent ones simply draped a dirty sheet over themselves and called it a costume.

Since it was customary for children of the period to do much of the family marketing, they knew the local shopkeepers well and were therefore in an excellent position to demand a handout in exchange for continued patronage. Uncooperative vendors "were rewarded by terrific and repeated bangings of the front door by the children," according to Smith. This specific prank was called "slamming gates," and the term also applied to the overall begging activity.

The rounds of the ragamuffins found antecedent and inspiration in New York's annual parades of "fantasticals," private clubs of adult men organized specifically to stage elaborate Thanksgiving costume parades. They functioned very much like the "krewes" still responsible for New Orleans's Mardi Gras. Both the fantasticals and krewes emerged about the same time in their respective cities, during the 1840s and 1850s. Thanksgiving historian Diana Karter Appelbaum describes the New York festivities as "a high-spirited extension of Guy Fawkes Day customs." As early as 1881, Thanksgiving in New York was attended by streets full of "robbers, pirates, fiends, devils, imps, fairies, priests, bishops, gypsies, flower girls, kings, clowns, princes, jesters – all in variegated and bewildering attire." Four years later, the tradition was still in full force, the *New York Times* reporting a "mass of moving, shouting beings, whose costumes were as varied as the whims of a coquette, dazzling the eye with the variegated brilliance of a kaleidoscope . . ."

Ragamuffins unofficially escorted the fantasticals through the streets. By the late 1920s the child revelers had eclipsed their elders in the quest for public attention and street space. In 1928, the *New York Times* covered the activities in the guise of a tongue-in-cheek theater review: "Yesterday's annual performance of the Metropolitan Child Mummers in 'Anythin' for Thanksgivin,' Mister?' made up in energy what it lacked in finesse. Playing to 'standing room only' in nearly every thoroughfare of the city, but concentrated primarily in the Times Square section, the cast was larger than usual, numbering, it was estimated by some, 12,747 in the boys' chorus and 2,839 girls." Blackface comedians and tramps were the most popular costumes. "Settings were urban, the décor modernistic," and "Financially the presentation made a new top."

The Macy's Thanksgiving Day Parade, first held in 1924, never had the expressed goal of suppressing ragamuffin antics, but, as its floats and balloons became increasingly eye-popping and media-centered, the event naturally attracted ever-larger and larger crowds, including crowds of children. The most spirited street dancing by a kid in a homemade costume was no competition for inflated corporate effigies of Felix the Cat, Mickey Mouse, or the Three Little Pigs.

The onset of the Depression brought Count Dracula to Hollywood prominence, but simultaneously struck a stake through the ragamuffins' collective heart. By 1932, New York schools were doing their part to officially discourage Thanksgiving begging, and the press lent its editorial support.

Time was – and not so very long ago – when all the streets were the gleeful haunts of the ragamuffin. Young men, with canes on one arm and girls on the other, were generous with dimes. Kindness was – in those pre-depression days – one of the major corollaries of love. Elderly gentlemen whose memories were dulled by too much turkey, port wine and sentiment gave lavishly . . .

Now, at the pit of the Depression, the formerly generous "had other uses for small change, since every penny is a pin feather on the chicken in the pot. Youth danced, clowned, begged, it ran vast uncertain races with the police – and all in vain. By mid-afternoon it had become all too clear that Thanksgiving was just Thursday."

But the ragamuffins had to go somewhere, and where they went was Halloween – in droves.

The new atmosphere of stinginess and need brought Halloween's always-percolating undercurrents of economic disparity, charity, and class resentment to a steady and significant simmer. A search through 1932 press accounts of Halloween pranks and vandalism in New York reveal no mention of anything resembling trick-or-treating, but tricks aplenty against private property and public safety. In Mount Vernon, a realistic dummy was dropped from a bridge onto the tracks in front of a speeding New Haven Railroad train. Luckily, there were no injuries. In Queens, an estimated four hundred street lamps were broken, windows were smashed "by the hundreds," and "surfaces of residences were seriously damaged, either by chipping of stucco or peeling of paint." Hints of class conflict emerge repeatedly in these accounts; one report took special notice that a car overturned by a "mass attack" of hoodlums was "a sedan of expensive make."

The stucco of America's social contract was likewise severely chipped by the time Franklin Roosevelt took office in 1933, and in a small way, the customs of Halloween pranking reflected more generalized anxieties about civil unrest. Ideas about alms, begging, and entitlements were no longer the stuff of a children's holiday. The economy had imploded in the wake of the 1929 Wall Street crash, nearly 20 per cent of American banks had failed, and increasing numbers of people were hoarding cash at home. President Herbert Hoover had sealed his political fate the previous year when twenty thousand unemployed or otherwise financially desperate veterans marched on Washington, demanding immediate payment of their World War I bonuses. The Bonus Marchers didn't get their treat, and were instead subject to a trick, forcibly ejected from their makeshift "Hooverville" encampments, which were then summarily, and ironically, burned under the direct supervision of a hero from the next war, General Douglas MacArthur.

Roosevelt's proposed "New Deal" of economic remedies struck many conservatives as tantamount to acceding to blackmail by Bolsheviks. The backlash against handouts to ragamuffins reflected the same controversy, though writ exceedingly small. And although Halloween never even registered in the national debate, the many local controversies surrounding the holiday echoed much larger political themes about anarchy, order, and wealth redistribution.

On Halloween 1934, the pranks of masked children parading through the streets of Harlem rapidly escalated from harmless flour and ash pelting to rock throwing to automobile vandalism. The police estimated that four hundred youngsters, both black and white, were involved in the various mêlées, which culminated with a car being heisted and rolled down a fifty-foot embankment in Riverside Park, where its tires were slashed. The same year, in New Britain, Connecticut, a wildly out-of-control Halloween celebration resulted in the death of a fourteen-year-old boy, who suffered a fractured skull and internal injuries after being beaten by a mob of twenty youths. The fact that the boy was the son of the city's deputy fire chief aroused a special amount of official alarm; the *New Britain Herald* went so far as to urge the mayor to request military protection for the following year. In nearby Monroe, Connecticut, the agonizing, fiery death of a six-year-old girl whose clothing was ignited by a Halloween-pumpkin candle did nothing to alleviate the general sense of unease surrounding the holiday, which, to many observers, seemed nothing but an invitation and excuse for social disaster. Fear of a seething underclass was a strong subtext of other reform movements of the early 1930s; film censorship campaigns, for example, got especially worked up about the Halloweenish content of horror and crime movies, each genre anarchic in its own way. Such entertainments were widely viewed as demoralizing threats to public order, October 31 all year long.

Old-fashioned ghosts were almost Halloween has-beens when they returned to the holiday as a popular obsession during the Jazz Age and Depression as millions were diverted each October by the titillating prospect of a return engagement by the spirit of Ehrich Weiss – better known during his mortal transit as Harry Houdini.

The escape artist/magician had been an international superstar before his death in Detroit on October 31, 1926. The previous week, Houdini had unwisely accepted a dressing-room dare from a university student and allowed himself be punched in the stomach. He may already have been suffering from undiagnosed appendicitis; the result was peritonitis and a swift but excruciating death. During his stellar career, Houdini had become almost as well known for debunking phony spiritualists as for his escape exploits. Interest in spiritualism had received a considerable boost from the monumental death toll of World War I, and Houdini reveled in exposing the techniques of mediumistic bunk. Nonetheless, less than a month after his demise, no less a publication than *Scientific American* reported a spirit-message from Houdini, supposedly received by a Massachusetts medium.

"Before he died," the *New York Times* reported, "he promised to communicate with persons on earth, if possible, for although he was skeptical of all phenomena he encountered and denounced most of it as fraud, he always hoped that it might be possible to communicate with those who had died." Houdini had made numerous compacts with persons whom he promised to contact after death, if such contact was possible. One was his wife, Bess; another was Sir Arthur Conan Doyle, an ardent spiritualist who had lost a son in the war and with whom Houdini had had a long and contentious relationship. To his wife alone he gave a code message, by which she would be able to determine whether any purported spirit-message was genuine.

Quite unlike her late husband, Bess Houdini was positively drawn to the occult. Houdini's niece, Marie Hinson Blood, recalled that "Aunt Bess could never pass a gypsy tent, or a palm or mind reader without going in for a reading."

For the first three Halloweens following her husband's death, Bess Houdini, awash in grief and alcohol, held private séances attended by prominent magicians; countless similar attempts to contact Houdini in the beyond were held around the country and around the world. If nothing else, the séances kept Houdini's name alive, the press happy, and the public fascinated. In 1930, Bess Houdini declared to the press that she had given up hope of making contact with her husband in the spirit world. But the announcement proved premature. A certain New York medium named Arthur Ford claimed that Houdini had communicated to him the words ROSABELLE ANSWER TELL PRAY ANSWER LOOK TELL ANSWER ANSWER TELL and the widow signed a statement acknowledging the message as her husband's code, even though she later expressed public doubts amid suggestions that the code was never quite the state secret it had been cracked up to be.

The widow found a new companion in Edward Saint, formerly a magician at the Rye Playland amusement park in New York. He was something of a showman, and adept at managing her business affairs – mostly hawking Houdini memorabilia, of which she had a warehouse full. Saint also assisted her with the Halloween séances for a decade. Finally, in October 1936, it was announced that there would be only one more official attempt.[7]

The séance was held at the Knickerbocker Hotel in Hollywood. Tinseltown was already more than primed for Halloween revels; Los Angeles-area nightclubs and restaurants advertised stylish indoor celebrations and all the beaches planned festive outdoor events, easily accessible by the city's extensive trolley system. PIXIES RIDE AGAIN TONIGHT, reported the *Los Angeles Examiner* at the top of page 1. "At all city playgrounds there will be general civic celebrations tonight, including fireworks, music, vaudeville and dancing – and independently there will be the usual horde of youngsters playing their pranks until collared and sent to bed." All in all, it was said to be "the most elaborate observance of Halloween" in Los Angeles history.

As *Time* reported the Houdini end of the story, "On the hotel roof, ignoring a milling throng of spiritualists, magicians, news-hawks, cameramen and gawkers, a plump, white-haired woman walked down a length of plush red carpet" and took her place at a table draped in red fabric. Arranged on the table were an enshrined photograph of Houdini, a pair of handcuffs, a silver bell, and a trumpet. Bells and trumpets were common props at séances, objects through which the departed might "speak." The handcuffs were

---

7. Nonetheless, Houdini Halloween séances have continued to the present day, with one of the latest versions officiated in the ectoplasmic realm of cyber-space.

Houdini's own, and only he might unlock them. The table was additionally stocked with other objects that a ghost might use to make noise or otherwise communicate: a tambourine, a slate board and chalk, paper and pencil, a blank-loaded pistol, and, finally, a candle purported to have been perpetually lit during the decade since Houdini's passing.

"The world is waiting," Saint intoned, "the entire world and your friends in the glamorous Hollywood you loved so much. Please speak, Harry . . . Call to him, Madam Houdini, call to him . . ."

After a period of crushing silence, Saint asked the widow for her final verdict. It came in a defeated voice, choked with emotion:

> I do not believe that Houdini can come back to me or to anyone. After faithfully following through for ten years the compact, using every type of medium and séance, it is now my personal and positive belief that spirit communication in any form is impossible. This light has burned for ten years. I now regretfully turn out the light. This is the end. Good night, Harry!

"She covered her face with her hands," wrote the reporter from *Time*. "The lights went up and the photographers crowded forward. In the street a Halloween fire-cracker exploded."

Sometime in the middle of the 1930s, enterprising householders, fed up with soaped windows and worse, began experimenting with a home-based variation on the old protection racket practiced between shopkeepers and Thanksgiving ragamuffins. Doris Hudson Moss, writing for *American Home* in 1939, told of her success, begun several years earlier, of hosting a Halloween open house for neighborhood children. "If the decorations are spooky enough, and if you provide food and a hearty welcome, you can be sure that the little rowdies from the other side of town will join in the party spirit and leave your front gate intact."

Moss reported that the children's grapevine system of communication worked very well, spreading the word that a sweet feast awaited all who would voluntarily refrain from mischief. She recalled "one gang of tiny lads who ate their late [meal] with too much relish and nearly broke my heart." These were the "other side of town" children, of course, once more reinforcing the sense that Halloween pranks amounted to small-scale class warfare.

The *American Home* article is significant because it is apparently the first time the expression "trick or treat" is used in a mass-circulation periodical in the United States. The kids from the wrong side of the tracks tiptoe onto Mrs. Moss's porch, intent on candle-greasing her windows, but

> to their surprise, they found our front door open and a jolly Jack o'lantern grinning from a window at them. Seeing me, they summoned nerve to speak the age-old salutation of "Trick-or-Treat!" When they learned that it was *treat* at our house they came smiling shyly into the dining room where other children were nibbling at doughnuts and sipping cider — and there were no *tricks*.

Moss's account is a bit puzzling, because she infers that the open house is both an innovation *and* something previously (and mysteriously) understood by children who are complete strangers. "Trick or treat" seems a fairly straightforward ultimatum, and it's hard to read a plausible alternative meaning. Moss also calls the "trick or treat" greeting "age-old," but hints at no particular antecedent or inspiration for her prophylactic party plan.

It is probable that trick-or-treating had its immediate origins in the myriad of organized celebrations mounted by schools and civic groups across the country specifically to curb vandalism. What works someplace is likely to be imitated someplace else; the grapevine of adult communication is usually just as efficient as the children's.

Paradoxes and conundrums aside, it does seem clear that the American custom of trick-or-treating, whatever its specific sources, inspirations, or influences, became widely known and adopted as a distinct property-protection strategy during the late Depression. The national spread of the custom, however, was not uniform. For instance, Cleveland kids in the 1930s blackened their faces with cork, paraded the streets, and knocked over garbage cans, but didn't go from door to door begging for nuts and candy. The holiday was all trick and no treat, perhaps befitting the somber zeitgeist of the Depression. The *Houston Chronicle* urged reform: '

> Halloween affords an excellent opportunity to civilize a holiday. As matters stand, it gives permit for unlicensed and unbridled mischief. It is an unregenerate sort of day needing redemption. The peculiar thing about the whole matter is that not much sport resides in its present observance, and almost anything which gave real punch and a carnival purpose to the holiday would have little competition from the present method in observation.

The *Chronicle* called Halloween "a day of loss to property owners, merchants, and even unwary passers-by, without affording its participants any real satisfaction. It can be reinterpreted in terms of a national carnival – an event which we really need in this country."

The new deprivations of World War II slowed reform and cast a national-security pall over previously tolerated pranking. In 1942, the Associated Press reprinted a letter from Rochester superintendent of schools James R. Spinning, addressed to his 38,383 students:

> Letting the air out of tires isn't fun any more. It's sabotage.
>
> Soaping windshields isn't fun this year. Your government needs soaps and greases for the war.
>
> Carting away property isn't fun this year. You may be taking something intended for scrap, or something that can't be replaced because of war shortages.
>
> Even ringing doorbells has lost its appeal because it may mean disturbing the sleep of a tired war worker who needs his rest.

It is the postwar years that are generally regarded as the glorious heyday of trick-or-treating. Like the consumer economy, Halloween itself grew by leaps and bounds. Major candy companies like Curtiss and Brach, no longer constrained by sugar rationing, launched national advertising campaigns specifically aimed at Halloween. If trick-or-treating had previously been a localized, hit-or-miss phenomenon, it was now a national duty. The begging ritual was modeled for millions of youngsters in the early fifties by Donald Duck's nephews Huey, Dewey, and Louie in Disney's animated cartoon "Trick or Treat," accompanied by a catchy, reinforcing song of the same title. Disney was also a leader in marketing costumes based on its popular characters, like Tinker Bell and Davy Crockett.

In a 1959 essay called "Halloween and the Mass Child," sociologist Gregory Stone expressed concern that Halloween had become "a rehearsal for consumership without a rationale" for postwar children. "Beyond the stuffing of their pudgy stomachs, they didn't know why they were filling their shopping bags." Stone interviewed eighteen Halloween visitors to his Missouri home.

Was the choice proffered by these eighteen urchins, when they whined or muttered, "Trick or treat?" or stood mutely at my threshold, a choice between production and consumption? Was I being offered the opportunity to decide for these youngsters the ultimate direction they should take later in life by casting them in the role of producer or consumer? Was I located at some vortex of fate so that my very act could set the destiny of the future? Was there a choice at all? No. In each case, I asked, "Suppose I said, 'Trick.' What would you do? Fifteen of the eighteen (83.3%) answered, "I don't know."

A minority of households did demand some kind of production or performance for the treat, harking back to the days of the Thanksgiving ragamuffins who would dance in the streets in exchange for a handout. One baby boomer, who grew up in St. Louis, can still remember his impatience with the neighbor who made each youthful petitioner tell a joke before receiving the treat. "One year we all told the same joke," he recalled. " 'What's green and wiggles?' 'Elvis Parsley.' "

But for many American kids in the fifties and sixties, Halloween had less to do with economic paradigms than with the expansive personal possibilities of the postwar era, a unique period in American history. Rochelle Santopoalo is a baby boomer who now edits *Happy Halloween* magazine for holiday enthusiasts. "There was the idea of being anybody you wanted to be," she says. "The question that was always posed around Halloween as a kid was, 'Who are you going to be?' It was always extremely liberating."

In the last few decades, the Halloween machine has been especially driven by boomers, a generation noted for a marked reluctance to give up the things of childhood. Halloween has now become its own economic paradigm, the largest holiday behind Christmas, and still growing. Precise figures are difficult to determine, but the annual economic impact of Halloween is now somewhere between four billion and six billion dollars, depending on the number and kinds of industries one includes in the calculations. According to the National Confectioners Association, candy alone accounted for two billion dollars in the year 2000. A similar amount is spent on costumes, and then there are the holiday decorations, theme-park revenues, seasonal movie, TV, and home video tie-ins, with all the attendant spending on advertising and promotion.

The neck-and-neck race between Christmas and Halloween was rather uncannily anticipated – and to a certain extent driven – by the immensely popular 1993 animated film *The Nightmare Before Christmas*, produced by Tim Burton and directed by Henry Selick. Beyond the imaginative entertainment values which rendered it an instant classic, the film speaks volumes about the essential interdependency of holidays. In 2001, Disneyland's popular Haunted Mansion attraction was re-outfitted for the yuletide season with the characters and imagery of *The Nightmare Before Christmas*. The Haunted Mansion thus metamorphosed into the Halloween machine itself – an eccentric, ever-evolving contraption, sometimes delightful and sometimes disturbing . . . but always a cause for celebration.

TWO

# THE WITCH'S TEAT

ITCHES, IT WAS ONCE believed by the good citizens of Salem, Massachusetts, could be readily identified by the presence of an uncanny extra nipple, or "witch's teat," from which they suckled their demonic "familiars" with human blood. A familiar could take the form of a cat, a toad, a rodent, or an insect; all were useful disguises enabling them to carry out the witch's mischief. The teat could appear most anywhere on the body, but was most often thought to provide its preternatural nourishment from the vicinity of the genitals or anus. Any birthmark or mole or flap of skin could be interpreted as a witch's teat, which made it an especially useful means of ferreting out witches, and gave prurient Puritans a handy justification for endless strip-searching, without the necessity for soul-searching.

To many observers today, the legacy of Salem's seventeenth-century witchcraft trials has itself become a kind of witch's teat, nourishing a modern, Halloween-centered growth industry catering to the public's bottomless fascination with witchcraft and the occult. Founded in 1981, Salem's "Haunted Happenings" celebration has grown into a month-long, major economic engine for the picturesque port on Boston's north shore, generating an estimated $30.3 million in direct local revenues (and $42.5 million if indirect impact is factored into the brew). With a population of just thirty-eight thousand, Salem attracts approximately one million visitors each year, nearly a quarter of whom swoop into town between the first week in October and Halloween. Not surprisingly, Salem proudly proclaims itself "The Witch City," with silhouettes of broomstick-riding hags emblazoned not only on a variety of tourist tchotchkes (coffee mugs, tote bags, and "kitchen witch" figurines are just the beginning of Salem-sanctioned souvenirs), but also on the official insignia of the Salem police department.

There are many large-scale Halloween celebrations throughout America, but none with Salem's duration and intensity. For example, a single wax-museum-style attraction might seem sufficient in most American cities, but Salem has a half dozen, including some with no apparent historical connection with Salem except for plain spookiness, like Dracula's Castle, the Vampire Vortex, and the Museum of Myths and Monsters. Boris Karloff's Witch Mansion owes more to Hollywood than to historical New England, but it still draws a crowd.

The august Peabody Essex Museum, repository of the original Salem witch trial documents, sponsors a lucrative series of "Eerie Events" featuring ghost stories told in "old, candlelit houses . . . Prepare to shiver!" These readings, involving, as they do, direct human communication unmediated by overt commercialism, authentically evoke an earlier age of oral folklore traditions, and are a welcome respite from aggressively frenetic attractions that tend to dominate "Haunted Happenings." The Salem Witches Magickal Arts Center hosts a fair featuring "Wiccan and Pagan vendors, herbal gift items, aromatherapy, jewelry, [a] magickal art exhibit, children's magick craft activities for ages 1 to 101," and an "Ask a Witch" information booth sponsored by the Witches Education Bureau. The Center also organizes an annual Samhain Feast to honor the Wiccan New Year (thirty-three dollars per person, with a polite request to "Wear your most magickal finery, nothing horrific or offensive.")

But, without question, the town's premier tourist destination is the Salem Witch Museum, a former church now housing vivid scenes of the witch trials and executions – most by hanging, but one by pressing under boards and boulders. A new group of tourists is ushered through every thirty minutes, year round, with the exception of Thanksgiving, Christmas, and New Year's Day. Around Halloween, tickets need to be purchased hours in advance. The tableaux are accompanied by dramatic recorded narration, music, and sound effects.

Following the main event, tourists exit directly into an extensive gift shop, stocking a wide assortment of witchcraft-related books, dolls and figurines, mulling spices for cider and wine, wind chimes, tarot cards, and videotapes on women and spirituality. A secondary exhibit, adjacent to the gift shop, is called "Witches: Evolving Perceptions," and presents a history of witchcraft skewed strongly to the prevalent New Age notion that witches were the victims of patriarchal oppression – nature-attuned midwives and healers who passed esoteric, goddess-derived wisdom from mother to daughter since pagan times. However, this may have more to do with Salem's present status as a mecca for Wicca than anything that actually happened in 1692.

"Salem's struggle between revenue for today and reverence for yesterday has become so touchy several people refused to go on record about the flourishing witch business," reported *USA Today* in 1997. "We don't have much of a tax base," admitted Salem witch Teri Kalgren. "Unless we want to sink, we have to do something."

Doing something means doing a lot, if the glut of Halloween activities in Salem is any indication. Accused witches in New England were subjected to grueling ordeals, but perhaps none so challenging as locating a parking space in modern Salem during a typical October weekend. With every lot and garage in the city filled to capacity, a visitor may well end up parking on a street a mile or more from the town center. But a leisurely stroll back to the commercial district gives one a good opportunity to gauge the depth to which Salem has become marinated in the macabre. Occult and New Age boutiques abound; some, like Crow Haven Corner ("Salem's First and Most Famous Witch Shop"), have substantial waiting lines, which probably justifies a certain redundancy among Salem vendors, at least during the October tourist season. Similarly, there's room for no less than five entrepreneurs to offer walking tours of Salem's haunted past, including narrated strolls through witch trial sites and historical burial grounds, with tales of "spectral assaults" and grisly crimes. Perhaps the most colorful tour description comes from Spellbound Tours' Vampire and Ghost Hunt, which seems to import elements of Transylvania to New England: "Join certified Ghost Hunter Mollie Stewart for a historical night-time walk around Salem's dark edges in search of the living dead! Visit a haunted cemetery, haunted buildings and a notorious murder site. Hear documented tales of New England vampirism and modern vampires!"

Just walking down the street, you're likely to be approached by a person in Victorian costume, offering to tell you a ghost story on the spot. There's a special costume parade for pets. Even the food in Salem offers a whiff of fantasy and brimstone. In addition to spooky dinner theater at Endicott Street's Mystery Café, the Crypt Café on Essex Street offers a "Tortured Turkey and Boursin Turnover," "Stephanie's Screaming Spinach Pie," and other taste treats, all to be washed down with the far mellower proposition of "Pumpkin Spice Coffee."

In the colonial summer of 1692, no one in Salem ate tortured turkeys, spinach didn't scream, and nobody had ever seen a wax museum. But the existence of the supernatural was an accepted fact of life, and twenty women and men of Salem were put to death for the crime of witchcraft. None knew anything about Halloween. Calvinist Puritans had little use for the Feast of All Saints or the Feast of All Souls, celebrations redolent of Rome and its rejected decadence. Since salvation and damnation were matters of predestination, there was little reason to commemorate saintly lives, much less pray for the souls of the dead. Good works on earth amounted to little more than a fruitless exercise in human vanity, and the dead, like the living, were beyond help anyway. God already knew who was lost and who was chosen. He had known from before the beginning of time and it was presumptuous for humanity to assume otherwise.

All Hallow's Eve, therefore, was of no importance to the Puritan colonists, who had established their own harvest celebration of Thanksgiving, an unofficial religious holiday that had nothing to do with the dead but everything to do with the relationship of the living to an inscrutable and terrifying Deity. Nonetheless, the ritual human sacrifice known as the Salem witch trials would ultimately take on the commercial patina of a festival whose purpose and meaning its victims would find utterly mystifying and, no doubt, abominable.

The incident at Salem began in the winter of 1691, when a niece and daughter of the Salem pastor Samuel Parris began to exhibit bizarre behavior. After frightening themselves with forbidden fortune-telling games, Abigail Williams and Betty Parris became subject to fits of babbling accompanied by strange physical contortions. Other girls became similarly afflicted, and soon the hysterical children were accusing neighbors and acquaintances of witchcraft. Among the first accused was the Parris's female slave, Tituba, who, on the advice of a neighbor, prepared a noxious "witch cake" made with the afflicted girls' urine – this, it was believed, might confirm the presence of a spell if fed to a dog (no canine reaction, negative or positive, has ever managed to find its way into the historical record). The slave Tituba ended up in shackles for her culinary zeal; the well-connected neighbor (the wife of a landowner) who provided the recipe got only a reprimand. The devil's methods could not be used even to combat the devil, it was argued. But, given what followed, it is clear that the most truly demoniacal energies in the whole affair would side with the accusers and not the accused.

More charges followed: The girls claimed they were being invisibly pinched and bitten by unpopular members of the community. More than two thirds of the condemned were women, some homeless, some senile, and more than a few had ongoing personal and property disputes. One, Bridget Bishop, had been accused twelve years earlier of casting spells and transforming herself into a cat. She had been acquitted then, but grudges had continued to fester. To the Puritan mind, interpersonal discord and worldly strife were a spiritual stain — unless, of course, they could be blamed on the devil.

The witch trials effectively exploded the blocked-up septic tank that was Salem's collective soul.

Arthur Miller, in his introduction to *The Crucible* (1953), the most celebrated dramatization of the trials,[8] aptly described the social dynamic:

8. Miller's play is rightfully considered a landmark of the American theater, though its fidelity to historical fact is another matter entirely. The adulterous relationship between John Proctor and Abigail Williams that forms the dramatic core of the play is entirely fictional. In a "Note on Historical Accuracy" in the first published edition, Miller admitted to increasing Abigail William's age for purposes of dramatic license. He failed to mention that the real Abigail was eleven years old and the real John Proctor was sixty; as historian Frances Hill comments in *The Salem Witch Trial Reader*, the two historical characters "probably never met except in court." The sexual twist made for gripping drama, however, and when Miller wrote the screenplay for the 1997 film adaptation, the sexuality was further amplified to include Winona Ryder cavorting nude in a witches' sabbath.

Long-held hatreds of neighbors could now be openly expressed, and vengeance taken, despite the Bible's charitable injunctions. Land-lust which had been expressed before by constant bickering over boundaries and deeds, could now be elevated to the arena of morality; one could cry witch against one's neighbor and feel perfectly justified in the bargain. Old scores could be settled on a plane of heavenly combat between Lucifer and the Lord; suspicions and the envy of the miserable toward the happy could and did burst out in the general revenge.

The accusing children's personal lives had been thrillingly transformed by the legal spotlight. Never again would they enjoy such attention, or such power. In *A Delusion of Satan* – the most lucid and nuanced of all the published trial accounts – Frances Hill paints a vividly bleak picture of the stifled existence that was a girl's typical fate in seventeenth-century Salem. "Their human urges to express their emotions, fulfill their desires, exercise personal will, and exert control over others were pushed out of sight. But, alas for Massachusetts, not destroyed."

A disproportionate number of the accused were enemies and land-rivals of the powerful Putnam family, whose daughter Ann had joined the chorus of possessed girls. Soon, Ann's mother (also named Ann) swelled their ranks further. Goodwife Putnam had had several stillborn children and wanted a reason; witchcraft provided the Puritan mind with acceptable explanations for infertility, crop failures, and livestock fatalities.

Nineteen were ultimately hanged from an oak tree at Gallows Hill in Salem Town. One contentious, litigious old man, Giles Corey, refused to stand trial and was summarily pressed to death under a pile of stones. One dog was hanged as well. Generally, those executed shared both a refusal to confess (no one who confessed to witchcraft was hanged) and some socioeconomic vulnerability. But as the afflicted girls became emboldened by the power and celebrity the community conferred upon them, their accusations began to overreach. When persons as illustrious as Cotton Mather and the wife of the governor of Massachusetts were denounced as witches, political steps were taken to bring the Salem hysteria to an end. But it was only the beginning of an American fascination with witchcraft that would find its most lasting repository in the iconography of Halloween.

The popular mythology of witchcraft had preceded Salem by centuries. The first graphic representations of the witch as a broomstick-riding crone date to Europe in the 1450s. Remarkably, the basic silhouette – peaked hat, ragged cloak, hooked nose – has evolved little between Renaissance woodcuts and today's Halloween decorations. An infamous 1486 tract by Heinrich Kramer and James Sprenger, the *Malleus Maleficarum*, was the first large-scale compendium of witchcraft lore and legend. Its authors were Dominican inquisitors, who had no doubt whatsoever about the veracity of the superstitions they cataloged. Its Latin title translating as "The Witch Hammer," the *Malleus Maleficarum* was published with the commission and blessing of Pope Innocent VIII as a handbook for recognizing, and smashing, witchcraft. By the fifteenth century witches had joined the ranks of persecuted heretics, and gave the Inquisition a shot in the arm that would propel it for another century.

Although some chroniclers of the European witch craze have claimed that millions of people, mostly women, were executed as witches, most serious historians believe the figure was one hundred thousand or fewer. However, women were disproportionately represented among the condemned, and the *Malleus Maleficarum* brims with misogynistic bile and endless warnings about female corruptibility. Some of the emphasis on female witches may have been just cynically practical: the Inquisition needed more victims, and women were simply less powerful, physically, economically, and politically.

Much traditional witch imagery, of course, conjures female domesticity: the broomstick, the kitchen cauldron-pot, and child–birth/midwifery – all transformed and demonized. "Normal" wo-men clean, cook, and nurture children; "witches" fly past the moon on their brooms, cook things other than food in their pots, suckle hellish animals, and use the fat of murdered infants to grease the transmissions of their broomsticks.

The witch's Halloween broomstick had a number of variant forms. In her coerced confession, Tituba of Salem said she flew to witches' meetings on an airborne pole. Pitchforks could work in a pinch, and more sedentary witches were apparently permitted to fly in chairs. And what fueled the aerial antics? Witches, according to the *Malleus Maleficarum*, employed an "unguent which . . . they make at the devil's instruction from the limbs of children, parti-cularly of those whom they have killed before baptism, and anoint with it a chair or broomstick; whereupon they are immediately carried up into the air . . ."

According to Freud, dreams and fantasies of flying are essentially sexual. The witch's broomstick, in its circumference and hardness, has a clear phallic symbolism, and was graphically depicted centuries before the insights of psychoanalysis. An illustration for the second edition of Pierre de Lancre's *Tableau de l'inconstance des mauvais anges et démons* (1612) shows witches cavorting lasciviously on brooms above a boiling cauldron; one of the major purposes of the witches' sabbath, of course, was sexual congress with the devil. In the Victorian era, witches were increasingly depicted as riding side-saddle, according to the corseted and decorous fashion of the time.

A high, brimmed black hat was a common feature of English country dress. To city-based illustrators and publishers, such hats may well have come to denote backwardness or eccentricity (this was certainly the case when Puritans, widely regarded as odd, adopted/adapted the hat as part of their own characteristic garb). More extreme, conical hats were linked to wizardry, alchemy, and heresy (as evidenced from paintings of the period, heretics were sometimes forced to wear conical hats at the time of their immolation); this image also informed the popular image of the witch. By providing an exaggerated, upward-reaching silhouette to the human head, these hats evoked extraordinary mental or occult powers, rising high above the capabilities of mere mortals. The thirteenth-century Scottish philosopher John Duns believed literally in the power of such hats, as witnessed by his celebrated invention, the Duns (or dunce) cap, originally intended to concentrate mental power in the intellectually challenged. Conical hats also appear in the iconography of fairy-tale princesses, elves, and other imaginative/magical beings. Generally and cross-culturally, headdresses often symbolize the higher powers of the mind and advanced or esoteric spirituality.

The official persecution of witches was reflected in art, drama, and literature almost from the beginning. As Candace Savage, author of *Witch: The Wild Ride from Wicked to Wicca*, observes, "When the witches in *Macbeth* first muttered into their cauldron on the stage of the Globe theater in 1611, real life 'witches' were dangling from gallows or writhing on pyres across western Europe." The eighteenth century saw witches and witchlike females appearing everywhere from the paintings of Goya to the fairy tales of Charles Perrault. Perrault's most famous creation, Mother Goose, fueled the image of the modern Halloween witch in her steady metamorphosis into a pointy-hatted crone sailing on broomsticks and attended by cats. By the mid-1800s Mother Goose was visually almost indistinguishable from the stereotypical witch, save for a benign disposition and a more colorful wardrobe. In Germany, the

Brothers Grimm revised their published tales with ever-darkening results, displayed most vividly in the terrifying cannibal-witch of "Hansel and Gretel," who originally had been a kindly old woman who gave the children refuge. In literature, she remains one of the wickedest witches of all time, a mother lode of misogyny, and a timeless evocation of the monstrous/maternal.

The New England witch-hunts were aided and abetted by European texts like the *Malleus Maleficarum*, and reinforced the misogynistic, witch-as-crone stereotype for the New World. According to historian John Putnam Demos, who closely analyzed the biographical characteristics of accused colonial witches in *Entertaining Satan: Witchcraft and the Culture of New England*, the typical witch was a female between forty and sixty years old (although Demos categorizes them as "middle-aged," life expectancies of the period were notoriously shorter than today – fifty was more than a ripe old age for many). Accused women tended to be of lower social rank, were prone to cantankerous neighborhood disputes, and often dabbled in healing and herbalism. Thus, they were already marginalized individuals with a preexisting whiff of the arcane. In short, they made perfect social scapegoats when scapegoats were needed.

The Salem witches were kept alive in opinionated post-trial tracts, such as Cotton Mather's absurdly credulous *Wonders of the Invisible World* (1693) and in more skeptical accounts like Thomas Hutchinson's *History of the Massachusetts Bay Colony* (1765). The Salem witches made their fictional debut rather tentatively, as part of a nonfiction preamble to John Neal's novel *Rachel Dyer* (1828). In 1835, Nathaniel Hawthorne published one of his best-known shorter works, "Young Goodman Brown," in which the title character, a fictitious resident of Salem in 1692, has a vision of a witches' sabbath involving most of the town's citizenry, including his own wife. The dark figure of the devil delivers a reality check to the congregation:

"Lo, there ye stand, my children," said the figure, in a deep and solemn tone, almost sad with its despairing awfulness, as if his once angelic nature could yet mourn for our miserable race. "Depending upon one another's hearts, ye had still hoped that virtue were not all a dream. Now are ye undeceived. Evil is the nature of mankind. Evil must be your only happiness. Welcome again, my children, to the communion of your race."

Whether the vision is real or a dream, it destroys Goodman Brown's faith in humanity forever.

Nathaniel Hawthorne himself had a family link to the Salem trials; his great-great-uncle, John Hathorne, was one of the presiding magistrates who had condemned Sara Good and others (Hawthorne changed the spelling of his surname to distance himself from the sins of his ancestor). On Gallows Hill, Goodwife Good angrily responded to a clergyman's last-minute request for a confession with what has come to be regarded as a curse: "I am no more a witch than you are a wizard, and if you take away my life, God will give you blood to drink." Legend has it that the clergyman later died of a throat hemorrhage. Hawthorne was haunted by his ancestral complicity in the Salem tragedy, and ultimately made it the foundation of his novel *The House of the Seven Gables* (1851). The titular house had a real model, still standing and another of Salem's most popular attractions.

Witches took to the stage in Engelbert Humperdinck's 1893 opera *Hänsel und Gretel* and in the turn-of-the-century fairy-tale illustrations of Arthur Rackham, popular in both England and America. The American children's author L. Frank Baum introduced the Wicked Witch of the West in *The Wonderful Wizard of Oz* (1900), though her appearance could not have been more different from the classic Halloween witch impersonated by Margaret Hamilton in the famous 1939 film. As depicted by the original

illustrator, W. W. Denslow, Baum's witch was a startlingly diminutive creature with ratty pigtails and a pirate's eye patch (her
remaining eye "was as powerful as a telescope, and could see
everywhere"), dressed almost festively in a towering striped hat,
a clownlike ruffled collar, a skirt decorated with frogs, snakes, and
moons, and shod – oddly enough – in spats.

It's not surprising that Hollywood opted for basic black. The
witch *noir* had long been winning out in popular iconography, and
by the turn of the twentieth century had been embraced as a
commercial icon by Salem, where it appeared sailing across the sky
in cosmetic "witch cream" advertisements and on picture postcards.
Salem itself had gone through a number of economic changes by
this time. At first a major port, Salem had become a manufacturing
and textile center, but as postwar suburban sprawl decentralized the
population and business, Salem's fortunes began to slump. But
before Salem would discover the profit potential of witches, popular
culture was doing much to reinforce the basic mythology.

After *The Wizard of Oz*, the witch became a stock cinematic icon,
celebrated in many popular films. In Rene Clair's *I Married a Witch*
(1942), Fredric March plays a New England politician romantically
bedeviled by a ghostly witch (Veronica Lake) whom his ancestors
consigned to the stake[9] three hundred years earlier. *Bell, Book and
Candle* (1958), adapted from the hit stage play by John Van Druten,
featured James Stewart and Kim Novak in another romantic supernatural comedy, an indirect but palpable precursor of the 1960s
television sitcom *Bewitched*. The dark side of witchcraft provided a
countervailing screen formula, invoked in films like *Horror Hotel*
(1962), in which the saturnine Christopher Lee, a warlock posing as
a college professor, sends a trusting young student to do research in a
Salem-like New England village, where she very nearly becomes a
footnote in the history of human sacrifice. *Rosemary's Baby* (1968),

9. In actuality, no witch was ever burned in New England.

directed by Roman Polanski from the bestselling novel by Ira Levin, reflected the shifting reproductive paradigms of the sexual revolution, transformed into a demonic struggle over a young woman's ability, or inability, to control her own pregnancy. A highlight of the film is a graphic depiction of a witch's sabbath in which Rosemary (Mia Farrow) is impregnated by the devil. The film received a "Condemned" rating from the Catholic Church, and was a key artifact in the late 1960s cultural upheaval over sex and censorship.

The countercultural movements of the 1960s had diverse origins, but mysticism and the occult were prominent threads. The Beatles weren't England's only cultural export of the period – the previous decade had seen the repeal of Britain's antiwitchcraft laws, and one previously closeted occultist, Gerald B. Gardner (1884–1964), openly founded a coven and published an influential book, *Witchcraft Today* (1954). Gardner claimed to be a member of an order of witches with an unbroken lineage to pagan times – a very dubious proposition, and one for which he provided no convincing documentation. Gardner was much indebted to the work of Margaret Alice Murray (1863–1963), an English anthropologist whose book *The Witch-cult in Western Europe* (1921) put forth the theory that witchcraft had its pagan origins in highly organized goddess worship and fertility rituals. She additionally maintained that the European witchcraft hysteria from the thirteenth through fifteenth centuries was a systematic purging of the old religion by Christian authority. Both Gardner and Murray have since been discredited by serious historians, who find neither documents or archaeological evidence to support their claims. Mainstream historians agree that some pagan customs and practices certainly persisted into the Christian era, but none really believe the myth of an underground, nature-based religion that has survived millennia. Nonetheless, the myth of the "old religion" had, and has, a powerful emotional appeal, especially for those seeking alternative spiritual paths.

Gardner called his religion "Wica," a spelling later standardized as "Wicca." The practice resonated strongly with burgeoning feminist and New Age movements, and Wicca was ensconced, along with tarot cards, the I Ching, and incense, as essential 1960s cultural décor. The "head shops" of three decades past are now most closely echoed in the offerings and accoutrements of the New Age, or Wiccan, boutique.

New England has always been fabled for its eccentrics, and Salem's witch history naturally began to attract religious iconoclasts. The counterculture of the 1960s and 1970s flourished on college campuses; the Boston area had (and has) one of the largest concentrations of educational institutions in the world. Wiccans began relocating to Boston's north shore, attracted by the "Salem" mystique and hoping for a tolerant environment. The commercialization of Salem witchcraft began in earnest in the early 1980s, when the Salem Witch Museum spearheaded a one-day "Haunted Happenings" celebration, which, depending on one's point of view, has been flourishing or metastasizing ever since. Like all religions, Wicca has a certain share of crackpots, but many more serious adherents in search of a religious practice free from the totalism and intolerance that are often a hallmark of establishment religion. In *Drawing Down the Moon*, journalist and practicing Wiccan Margot Adler sums up the gulf:

Most fundamentalists do not believe this world, this earth, these bodies we inhabit are holy. Since they see this world as sinful and this time as evil, they seek only a world that comes after. Several hundred years ago, the Inquisitors felt they were acting with the greatest human kindness when they tortured, burned, and hanged those they called "Witches" in order that their souls might be saved. They are not so different from their descendants . . . who wistfully yearn for salvation, even if it takes the form of nuclear war.

Unfortunately, such nuanced insights don't usually attract the media, which prefers its modern witches in outlandish robes and pentagrams, and, whenever possible, in some noisy conflict with traditional religious folk, where not much of anything is communicated. As a result, the public face of witchcraft in Salem soon had very little connection to real religious issues, and everything to do with commercial hype.

In 1991, a group of five Massachusetts filmmakers – Joe Cultrera, Henry Ferrini, Phil Lamy, Bob Quinn, and John Stanton – began work on *Witch City*, the first documentary look at the macabre Disneyfication of Salem. The project had begun as a fictionalized screenplay about Salem's history's impact on its modernity – an update, in its own curious way, on the theme of Nathaniel Hawthorne's *House of the Seven Gables* – but in the end, reality itself proved too strange to resist.

Cultrera, who narrated and edited the video, is a Salem native who has fond memories of his postwar Salem childhood: small-town civic celebrations that never needed to evoke images of horror and execution; tightly knit ethnic neighborhoods, a high school football team without witches emblazoned on its helmets, and ice cream stands that weren't called "Dairy Witch."

*Witch City* begins with a quote from Nathaniel Hawthorne: "If we look through all the heroic fortunes of mankind, we shall find this same entanglement of something mean and trivial with whatever is noblest in joy or sorrow." The documentary lets the dichotomies speak for themselves as merchants, tourists, and clergy (traditional and nontraditional) voice their opinions on Salem's Halloweenization.

Says Salem mayor Neil Harrington, "The fact of the matter is that shopping malls have stolen the productivity away from more traditional downtowns like Salem. It's a changing time, and Salem has to adapt and adjust. And one of the things is to use our assets and use our strengths and to use the things they can't take away from us."

Bif Michaud, owner of the Salem Witch Museum, denies that his venue unduly exploits Salem's tragic past. "We don't commercialize it at all," he explains. Instead, "We give people, we give [the] public what it wants." He also invokes Nazi atrocities as a model for considering the Salem story. "Salem in 1692 is no different than the Holocaust in 1942. Is it any more important to lose nineteen of those lives on Gallows Hill or six million lives in Europe? In any case, they're dead."

Wiccan entrepreneur Laurie Cabot, very much alive and Salem's most mediagenic pagan, explains that she originally came to Salem to avoid religious discrimination: "Wearing traditional witch's robes all the time, I found it difficult to work at IBM." Cabot complains about stereotypical witches' green faces, but personally doesn't shy away from video-friendly black robes, exaggerated eye makeup, and a mass of lightning-streaked hair.

*Witch City* also spotlights the 1992 unveiling of Salem's Witch Trials Memorial, an event given special gravitas by the presence of both Nobel Peace Prize winner Elie Wiesel and *Crucible* playwright Arthur Miller. In his official remarks, Wiesel denounces religious fanaticism, which he very correctly identifies as a real evil in the modern world. But when approached by a *Witch City* interviewer to comment on the commercial trivialization of the Salem legacy, he dodges the point entirely. "Who am I to criticize tourism?" Wiesel asks.

Miller is similarly caught off guard when asked to comment on souvenir samples of Gallows Hill dirt being hawked by a local businessman. He shakes his head slightly, but it is impossible to determine whether he is simply declining comment or registering an opinion.

"If truth is the first casualty of war, history is often the first casualty of commerce – in America, anyway," began the *Boston Globe's* review of *Witch City*. "What makes the low-budget documentary so watchable is its zesty comic style, which remains bouncy even when the humor gets scabrous," wrote reviewer John Koch.

Salem itself was not so amused. According to producer Quinn, a scheduled premiere of *Witch City* at the Peabody Essex Museum was canceled because of local merchants' objections. An alternate location was found, and the documentary was later aired on Boston's public television station WGBH and subsequently on other public stations across the country, and is now available on video.

*Witch City* captures in vivid microcosm the rise of confrontational Christian fundamentalism in America, its wrath here directed at Salem's neopagans, who seem to serve as social shorthand for just about anything that raises evangelical ire. In a Christian anti-Halloween parade, a bleeding Jesus is tied to a crucifix mounted on a flatbed truck emblazoned with the beer-inspired slogan THIS BLOOD'S FOR YOU. The Wiccans respond with their own street demonstrations, arguing that their religion is nature-based and has nothing to do with the Christian God, much less Satan. Nonetheless, they can't seem to resist wearing the kind of gothic cowls and capes that might have made Aleister Crowley proud.

Satanism exploded across the American landscape in the 1980s as witchcraft (that is, the *Malleus Maleficarum* variety) became a lurid mainstay of high-profile child-abuse prosecutions, tabloid television, and – not incidentally – Halloween bashing. The cultists' reputed ritual transgressions extended beyond sexual abuse, typically including flamboyant acts of animal sacrifice, incest, infanticide, blood drinking, and cannibalism. It was a matter of faith among the accusers that the individual crimes were part of a larger, highly organized satanic conspiracy. A large percentage of the cases turned on testimony developed from recollections accessible only through hypnosis. Skeptical commentary on these new witch trials was surprisingly scant, but, when it appeared, the legacy of Salem was usually invoked, explicitly or implicitly. Elizabeth Loftus and Katherine Ketcham, leading critics of the "recovered memory" movement, commented on the especially bizarre case of an Olympia, Washington, deputy sheriff, Paul Ingram, who is now serving a twenty-year prison sentence after pleading guilty to practicing satanic ritual abuse on his daughter for seventeen years. In this case, both the accusation and the confession were the products of visions experienced in hypnotic trances, with no corroborating evidence − essentially the same thing as the subjective "spectral evidence" allowed at the Salem trials. According to Loftus and Ketcham, "The investigation rapidly spiraled into hysteria, evoking memories of an earlier time when God-fearing citizens, gripped by fear, superstition, and religious fervor, cried witch, and a forest of stakes was pounded into the very heart of the community."

On Halloween 1994, the *New York Times* reported the results of the first empirical study refuting the existence of satanic cults. The report was based on a University of California at Davis survey of 6,910 psychiatrists, psychologists, and clinical social workers, as well as 4,655 district attorneys, police departments, and social service agencies. The survey participants reported a total of 12,264 investigated cases of purported satanic abuse, none of which uncovered even a single instance of satanic conspiracy. At best, there were a handful of cases in which lone perpetrators or couples injured children against cheesy, media-driven backdrops of black robes and inverted crucifixes. But these rare exceptions only proved the rule: the real evidence for an organized network of devil worshipers preying on American children was absolutely nil.

"There are, of course, people who will be unswayed by this new study because of their belief that abusive satanic groups do exist but are successful at eluding detection," wrote *Times* reporter Daniel Goleman.

Not surprisingly, Halloween figured prominently in the conspiracy claims. To the believers in satanic cults, the holiday was, and is, an open invitation to an orgy of human and animal sacrifice – a kind of Super Bowl for the 666 set. Nowhere is this vision more graphically depicted than in the comic book tracts of the singular Jack T. Chick. His publishing empire based in a nondescript storefront in Rancho Cucamonga, California, Chick runs statistical rings around publishing superstars like Stephen King and Tom Clancy. If estimates of his sales figures are accurate, his more than 450 million publications in print make him the most widely read author of all time.

Granted, Chick's publications aren't exactly full-length books; instead, they're twenty-four-page pamphlets of a size that can almost be secreted in the palm of one's hand. Reportedly, Chick was impressed by the effectiveness of comic tracts in disseminating propaganda in Communist China, and adapted the technique for his own purposes. Since the 1960s, Chick has inveighed against Catholicism, Mormonism, Darwinism, homosexuality, abortion, feminism, satanism, and, of course, Halloween.

In his 1986 tract "The Trick," Chick introduces a blond, black-robed baddie named Sister Charity during a crucial pre-Halloween planning session with other satanists. All the assembled wear menacing cowls; candles, a pentagram, and a skull are chillingly visible. The windows, of course, are mullioned. Sister Charity reminds her cohorts that Halloween is an important, sacrificial holiday. "Sacrifices are necessary for our cleansing," she explains. Razor blades, crushed glass, and other sharp objects are to be placed in children's treats; additionally, poisons and drugs will be injected into candy to assure the requisite mortality. And to make an evil outcome triply sure, incantations and curses are intoned over the goodies, the better to "influence the children eating them."

Flash forward to Halloween night. Despite references to the unspecified but apparently dire fate of a neighborhood youngster the previous year, Johnny Dexter's mother nonetheless allows him to don a devil costume. But her strict admonition that the boy restrict his begging to neighbors he knows on his own block for a period not to exceeed one hour does nothing to save him. One of Sister Charity's devilish cohorts, Miss Brenda (a brunette), is well known to the children, and is ready with her booby-trapped confections when Johnny and his friends (dressed as a witch and a ghost) arrive on her doorstep. The unholy three partake of a terrible communion, and the next stop is the emergency room. Johnny Dexter is dead, Susie is in intensive care, and Jerry is undergoing surgery to repair mouth lacerations.

Sister Charity toasts the local news broadcast reporting the atrocity, certain that Satan will appreciate her efforts. Instead, he gives her a fatal heart attack. What of the promise that she would rule with Satan in hell for her evil deeds? "Haw, haw, haw!" replies the Prince of Darkness. The "stupid little fool" was only getting her just deserts. "My *trick* was getting you to serve me. Now your *treat* is to burn for eternity." Satan has an imposing, body builder's silhouette, dramatically delineated against the flames of hell.

Despite the limited range of Johnny Dexter's trick-or-treating on the night of his death, Miss Brenda somehow never comes under suspicion. Ten months later, the children who survived the Halloween holocaust are rebelliously uncontrollable. Becky, a visiting former witch who now serves Jesus, diagnoses the problem and explains (erroneously) that trick-or-treating was an invention of the druids, who went from home to home on Halloween demanding sacrificial children or virgins. Those who cooperated would receive a jack-o'-lantern (illuminated by a candle rendered from human fat) that would protect the household against demonic onslaught. Those who refused would have the sign of a pentagram emblazoned on their doors, a signal for demons to summarily slay an inhabitant.

The ex-witch Becky quickly persuades the mothers of the afflicted children to accept Christ as their Lord and Savior. Miss Brenda steals away, muttering curses, and the children are restored to God.

Shortly before my Halloween visit to Salem – the locale of the satanic "Salem High" in another Chick tract, "Boo!" (1991) – I began researching Salem's wider reputation among Christian fundamentalists, and quickly came across "Child Sacrifice in the New Age: Salem's Witch Cult and America's Abortion Industry," an online article written by pro-life activist Jay Rogers, a Massachusetts native who worked in the Salem area for several years. "Salem, Massachusetts not only symbolizes witchcraft to tourists with a casual historical interest," he writes, "but is the national headquarters of an organized, politically-active and profitable cult." In fact, Salem's neopagans are only loosely affiliated, but Rogers attributes to them the hierarchical discipline and political zeal which far better characterize right-wing activists.

Rogers argues that abortion's origins are essentially occult, the modern residue of sacrificial rites dating to Celtic prehistory. He also suggests that the Salem witches of 1691 might not have been as innocent as most historians maintain, and were likely baby killers. There is nothing whatsoever in the historical record of the Salem trials that even hints at this, but other Web links amplify the witchcraft/abortion argument, which unpleasantly echoes the ancient blood libel against the Jews, who were believed to murder Christian babies for use in Passover rituals. A related strain of Web sites, tracts, and videotapes finds similar pagan/satanic conspiracies in heavy metal music and in Hollywood. Time and again, the name *Salem* is invoked as a locus of devilish depravity, a lurid example of where America is wrongheadedly heading.

Obviously, Salem's enthusiastic embrace of the supernatural makes it a tempting target for religious zealots. So does the fact that Salem has one of the largest per capita populations (however diverse) of practicing neo-pagans anywhere in the world – an estimated twenty-five hundred out of a total population of thirty-nine thousand. And, not surprising, many of the practitioners – independent, liberal, and otherwise iconoclastic women – happen to be pro-choice. If the right has a well-established flair for demonizing the left, in Salem the demonization is literal.

The fundamentalists have a special beef with the aforementioned Laurie Cabot, the self-advertised "official witch" of Salem, despite the town's formal refusal to designate a single "person or spirit" as a figurehead witch. In 1977, Cabot circumvented town officials by appealing directly to then-Governor Michael Dukakis and success-fully obtained a Massachusetts Patriot's Award, for community activities including work with dyslexic children. Although the archaic citation came with few tangible benefits (except the du-biously valuable rights to graze cattle on the Boston Commons and to wear a special tricorn hat), the language did include the "official witch" designation that Cabot coveted. In 1988, Dukakis's flustered presidential election team flatly denied that the executive order was ever signed, despite evidence to the contrary. A witch as canny as she is uncanny, Cabot has flown the title proudly in her promotional materials ever since.

On one level, a trip to Salem does seem to present the visitor with an evangelical Christian nightmare, one that religious activists seem to have given up as a lost cause, at least during a sunny Saturday preceding Halloween. In October 2000, the Revered Kenneth

Stiegler, pastor at the Wesley United Methodist Church, raised more than ten thousand dollars and conscripted local seminary students to distribute fifty thousand anti-Halloween tracts to Salem pilgrims. But in the course of my own visit a year later, I saw only one, slightly discombobulated Christian pamphleteer, largely ignored by the swirling eddies of pedestrians in swift pursuit of the pagan. However, it doesn't take an extremely cynical point of view to conclude that both the Wiccans and Christians are engaging in a bit of mutual back-scratching each October, giving the media what it wants and keeping themselves squarely in the spotlights of their choice.

There is little sign of Halloween fatigue in Salem. Instead, the glut of activity engenders a spirit of competition. "Tired of tacky tourist traps?" advertises one New Age boutique. "Come to Sacred Space . . . Where the True Craft Survives." Too many wax museums? The Boris Karloff Witch Mansion trumps all others with its exclusive 3-D visual effects. Like the townsfolk of "Young Goodman Brown," modern Salemites have tapped into a bottomless community well of black magic and discovered an abundant capacity to turn lore into gold.

But Halloween does take its toll in small ways. Late in the day, at Dracula's Castle, "Salem's Oldest and Largest Haunted House," on Lafayette Street, the gatekeeper acknowledges the price he must pay. He's twenty-something, wearing a regulation vampire tux and cape, but after sunset has traded in his patent-leather opera pumps for an incongruous pair of sneakers. Asked about the sartorial gaffe, he shrugs philosophically, while waving another group of visitors into the mouth of hell. "After eight hours on my feet, man . . . it's gotta be Nikes."

# THREE

# HOME IS WHERE THE HEARSE IS
## *Or, How to Haunt a House*

HE PLAYBOY MANSION is usually associated with ample endowments of the flesh, but one night of the year the *Playboy* aesthetic is turned autopsy-turvy, and bodacious bosoms collide with rotting, skeletal rib cages.

The last Saturday night in October is Hugh Hefner's annual Halloween bash, drawing an exclusive Hollywood crowd of over a thousand to his Holmby Hills estate, transformed for the evening into an unusually posh chamber of chills. If there is a larger or more elaborate private haunted house anywhere in the world, no one has yet come forth to claim the title.

A few days before the 2001 event, I am given a backstage tour by Rich Correll, who has handled arrangements for Halloween chez Hefner for several years. Correll is a TV sitcom director and a major collector of horror and sci-fi memorabilia, a good deal of which is incorporated as décor for the Playboy bash. In addition to this event, Correll also decks out the exterior of his Hancock Park home as a Halloween drive-by attraction.

The entry hall to the Playboy Mansion is transformed into an impressively macabre trophy room, with hundreds of horror masks glowering down from the darkly paneled Tudor walls. Outside, the grounds are given over to walk-through, animatronic corridors of zombies, skeletons, and the hungry dead. The displays are state-of-the-art, the sort of exhibits one would ordinarily encounter only at a highly capitalized theme park.

To turn the Playboy Mansion into a spook house costs around five hundred thousand dollars – these days the low-end price for a breathing person's bungalow in one of Los Angeles's better neighborhoods. The juxtaposition of conspicuous consumption with chastening images of mortality immediately brings to mind medieval woodcuts of the Dance of Death, where frisky, skeletal corpses make a mockery of materialism, vanity, and the pleasures of the flesh.

The classic Dance of Death, as delineated by Hans Holbein the Younger and others, was partly a response to the mass plague devastation of the Middle Ages. The public's appetite for stylized encounters with images of death has always been whetted by troubled times. Following the French Revolution, wax modeler Marie Tussaud (1761–1850) captivated a politically wary Europe with replicas of guillotined heads she had been forced to mold from the genuine articles upon threat of her own beheading. In the guise of historical education, modern-day visitors to Tussaud's London museum can still see, on pikes, original casts of the bloody heads of Louis XVI and Marie Antoinette (their shorn hair respectfully restored) along with what is purported to be the very blade that decapitated them. Though most of her output consisted of genteel three-dimensional portraiture, by the end of her life Tussaud's name was virtually synonymous with the phrase *Chamber of Horrors*, first coined by the British magazine *Punch* in 1845.

Morbid spectacle was also a major drawing card of Victorian London's Bartholomew Fair, which attracted patrons with displays of deformity and disease. Joseph Merrick, better known as the Elephant Man, was the most celebrated human anomaly thus presented. In America, P. T. Barnum was frustrated in his attempts to bring Tussaud's waxworks to New York, but his American Museum institutionalized the freak show as a viable economic model. The more gruesome aspects of modern Halloween attractions were vividly anticipated by the Eden Musée in New York City, both a waxworks and a theater, which lovingly re-created the details of early-twentieth-century ax murders and other crimes for patrons who otherwise could rely only on the verbal descriptions of crudely printed tabloids for their death fix. Some of the last remaining Eden Musée exhibits were displayed at the Cedar Point amusement park in Sandusky, Ohio, during the 1960s; even the most extreme Halloween presentations of the present day are unlikely to re-create the Eden Musée's lurid tabloid tableaux, including children with their heads half hacked off. The Musée's artisans had an especially disturbing talent for creating convincingly dead yet staring eyes, which focused almost pornographically on unsuspecting visitors as they turned a corner. One can only wonder what the Eden Musée would have done with Sharon Tate, Nicole Simpson, or JonBenet Ramsey.

Even more unnerving than the Eden Musée was the Theatre du Grand Guignol of Paris. Founded in 1897, the theater derived its name from the traditional *guignol*, or puppet show. The "big" *guignol* was a showcase for human variations on the classic Punch-and-Judy formulas, which included abrupt shifts from comedy to violence. The Grand Guignol repertoire drew theatrical energy from the despairing social tenets of naturalism but rapidly evolved its own brand of graphic, Sadean melodrama. Human actors got knocked around with the same abandon as the Punch and Judy characters, only now they bled. The resourceful technicians of the Grand Guignol rose to the challenge, developing an arsenal of realistic illusions by which actors could be stabbed, hacked, skinned, blinded, and mutilated onstage. It seems to have run into trouble with the authorities only when it attempted to depict the actual workings of the guillotine. Wax museums waned as mainstream institutions in the early twentieth century; their holdings were relocated and marginalized to venues like Coney Island, home to the remnants of the Eden Musée until well after the end of World War II. Like classic wooden roller coasters, creepy fun houses and "dark rides" were firmly ensconced at American parks by the 1930s, providing cheap thrills to a Depression-staggered public. The motorized "Laff in the Dark" ride, in which a swiveling passenger car followed a single, sinuous track, was far more likely to include macabre, pop-up images of skeletons, devils, and witches, though the traditional fun-house maze would also provide ample inspiration to future generations of Halloween attractions.

Publications offering advice on hosting Halloween parties during the thirties and forties often suggested the use of fun-house techniques at home, especially dark walkways where celebrants were invited to handle wet, slimy objects meant to represent human eyeballs, brains, and viscera. In reality, these would be peeled grapes and congealed masses of cold pasta, chicken giblets, and the like. In a pinch, of course, a blindfold could be effectively substituted for a dark basement. In an uncharacteristically nasty 1948 short story, "The October Game," Ray Bradbury epitomized the practice, with a Grand Guignol finish. "The witch is dead, and this is her head," intones a not-so-nice father at his daughter's Halloween party, and begins to pass around a variety of objects, all grisly to the touch. The children shriek with delighted alarm, until somebody finally realizes that the daughter is not in the room. Or seems not to be. "Then . . ." the story concludes, "some idiot turned on the lights."

The American spook-house experience has a strong atmosphere of ritual initiation, with faux-gruesome ordeals curiously akin to the rumored membership rites of secret societies. The classic haunted house is a gauntlet to be run (or ridden, in the case of the dark ride), a controlled confrontation with forces of darkness from which one emerges triumphantly unharmed, renewed, and bonded with one's companions. In short, a classic success story. A "house," of course, is also an especially elastic and evocative symbol of the self, not to mention the premier American icon of material security. The rise of the haunted house as a persistent American institution, however, suggests a basic ambivalence about the materialist ethos. On one level, the spook house respiritualizes an increasingly secularized consumer culture, even if only at Halloween. Ghosts, zombies, and other revenants may amount to quaint pop shorthand for a certain missing dimension in modern life. In America, if one's home is one's castle, then a haunted castle may be even better.

The gold standard for haunted houses was firmly established in 1969 with the introduction of one of Disney's most popular theme-park attractions, the Haunted Mansion. With versions at Disney-land, Walt Disney World, Tokyo Disney, and Disneyland Paris (where it is known as the Phantom Manor), the Haunted Mansion combines aspects of the traditional ghost train with a degree of technological wizardry never before attempted or achieved. The attraction had an extremely long period of development. Report-edly, Disney started tinkering with the idea in 1951, when Disney-land itself was on the drawing boards. Early concepts revolved around the Halloween-themed Disney animated short film, "The Legend of Sleepy Hollow," half of the 1949 feature *Ichabod and Mr. Toad* (the other sequence, based on *The Wind in the Willows*, was already the basis for one of Disneyland's original attractions, Mr. Toad's Wild Ride). The original façade of the Disneyland Haunted Mansion, an antebellum architectural fantasia located in the park's New Orleans Square, was completed in 1962, creating substantial anticipation over several seasons for the finished attraction. Disney himself didn't live to see his pet project come to fruition – he died in 1967 – but fans weren't disappointed when the Mansion finally creaked opened its doors, two months before Halloween 1969. Disney himself made no postmortem appearance in the attraction, though a bizarre, back-from-the-dead urban legend almost immediately took hold upon Disney's demise. Disney, it was whispered, had his body – or, in some variations, just his head – cryogenically frozen for future resuscitation. In reality, Disney was cremated.

Walt Disney believed in the technological perfection of America, and haunted houses were no exception. Riding in comfortable trains of stereo-speaker-equipped "doombuggies," visitors to the Haunted Mansion pass through a series of stunningly realized techno-tableaux, including a graveyard, a séance parlor with the disembodied head of "Madame Leota" speaking to visitors from within a crystal ball, marble statues that come to life, and, most spectacular of all, a cobwebby ballroom full of dancing, transparent phantoms. Some of the effects involve state-of-the-art animatronics and interior projection; others, like the ballroom illusion, are based on simple but highly effective tricks involving the careful calibration of glass reflections, a technique first developed for nineteenth-century stage presentations of Marley's ghost in *A Christmas Carol*.

The Haunted Mansion is a year-round attraction, but its phenomenal success and positive word of mouth seems to have brought the public's interest in seasonal haunted houses to a creative critical mass. Since few individuals or organizations had the resources of the Disney company, money and energy naturally gravitated to the obvious time of the year for likely success: Halloween.

Bob Burns, one of the best-known collectors of vintage memorabilia from classic films of fear and fantasy, was among those keenly anticipating the Haunted Mansion's debut when he began to take Halloween into his own hands in the late 1960s. Burns was born in 1935 in Oklahoma, where he vividly remembers begging from door to door in a makeshift ghost costume at the age of five. But he also distinctly recalls that the phrase "trick or treat" was unknown in Oklahoma during the Depression; he only encountered it when his family moved to southern California during World War II.

There weren't too many commercial Halloween costumes available in those days, but the Disney company was ahead of the game, and Bob's first Halloween costume in California was Mickey Mouse, an old-fashioned model with the mask fashioned from cheesecloth. His school encouraged kids to wear costumes to school on Halloween – in all likelihood, an example of the nationwide movement by schools and civic groups to channel potential Halloween mischief into controlled celebrations. "I was very shy in school," remembers Burns. "I didn't make friends easily, I had my heavy Oklahoma accent so I got kidded all the time," but the Halloween he wore the Mickey Mouse outfit, he was transformed into Mr. Popularity. "I became like the Pied Piper. Every kid in school followed me all over the place. It was very weird. People loved it."

Burns grew up in Burbank, and close proximity to the film studios fostered an interest in movies. He befriended many personalities of 1940s serials and 1950s B-pictures, and himself ended up playing one of the cabbage-headed aliens in *Invasion of the Saucer Men* (1957). By the 1960s, he had amassed a large number of props, masks, and memorabilia from Saturday-matinée-style films. Even before the 1974 Houston trick-or-treat poisoning of eight-year-old Timothy O'Bryan, and the later Tylenol tampering panic, much of the bloom had already worn off the American Halloween ritual. Baseless urban legends about random candy booby-trapping were already taking root, and nearly two decades of television had transformed the culture, isolating members of previously interactive communities. The news brought home by television did its part to engender social mistrust: the Kennedy assassinations, the divisive politics of the Vietnam War, and the weird media spectacle of hippies and love children curdling into Charles Manson and his macabre, homicidal "family." It was therefore not at all surprising that trick-or-treaters were no longer welcome *inside* people's houses, and even treats made at home were regarded warily.

Bob and his wife, Kathy, were both concerned about the decline in traditional Halloween spirit when they put on their first Halloween show in 1967. It consisted of turning their living room into Frankenstein's laboratory. Bob had a mask of actor Glenn Strange, who had played the monster in three Universal films, and fabricated a full dummy body, strapped to an upright operating table. An oversize portrait of Bela Lugosi as Dracula glowered over the proceedings. "I had a Jacob's ladder going," Burns recalls, "and a lot of blinking lights. I recorded the zaps off the soundtracks of one of the movies, so we had that, too." Kathy Burns wore a shroud and grimly distributed the obligatory candy, but the laboratory was the real treat. The tableau ended when Bob, hidden behind the door in a Neanderthalish Mr. Hyde mask, jumped out and scattered the screaming trick-or-treaters – making room, of course, for a new batch.

Encouraged by neighborhood response, in 1968, the Burnses staged another event. Kids who had never seen the couple's actual living room now were invited to see it as a traditional cobwebbed, haunted manse, with ingenious ghost projections undulating on the walls. And once more Bob put on one of his monster heads and hid behind the door to give the kids a final, scarifying "boo."

Soon, Halloween became an occasion for Burns to pay tribute to classic science fiction films of the 1950s that had been produced at the nearby studios. In the days before the home video revolution and the burgeoning of repertory cinemas, old B-movies were not easily accessible to the general public, except through the unpredictable caprice of local television stations. In the absence of view-on-demand, the reputation and mystique of these films were kept alive primarily in a slew of avidly read monster magazines (professional and amateur), and in home-grown, hands-on happenings like those staged by Bob Burns at Halloween. For his 1969 homage to Universal's 1954 science fiction film *This Island Earth*, he retrofitted his living room as the interior of a flying saucer, complete with a bulge-brained alien mutant. After Hollywood discovered science fiction, its imagery became ever more death-evocative. The mutant from the planet Metaluna in *This Island Earth* wore its skeleton on the outside, its swollen head resembling nothing so much as a psychedelic skull. The "little green man" Halloween mask, occasionally seen in the sixties and seventies, would soon be supplanted by the skeletal/fetal, hollow-eyed "alien abductor" as a favorite holiday disguise. An informal canvassing of local Halloween stores in 2001 made it clear to this writer that the alien was beating out the traditional skeleton as a Halloween bogeyman, the costumes sometimes including Grim Reaperish cowls and capes. Americans sometimes seem as terrified by technology as death, and the space alien assigns a special Halloween face to this hybrid anxiety.

In any event, space spooks only increased the appeal of Burns's exhibit. There was no returning to jack-o'-lanterns and black cats. The crowds swelled, word of mouth grew, and it was obvious that the limited portal of Burns's front door was no longer going to be adequate to meet public demand.

Accordingly, the next year's attraction raised the ante from living room decoration to street theater. Burns and a talented team of technicians built a huge, one-eyed, many-armed alien and plopped him squarely on top of the house. The monster's name was Goombah. "He had big tentacles that went out over the yard, and when you looked inside the door, it seemed like the house was wrecked. We made the ceiling looked crashed in and he had a victim, with one of the Goombah's tentacles wrapped around him, and he was groaning and screaming and everything." Atop the house, a pair of puppeteers inside Goombah manipulated the tentacles and moved the cyclopean eye to hungrily follow trick-or-treaters along the street.

Kathy Burns was relieved when the show moved completely out

of the house in 1971. Twelve hundred visitors turned out for "The Return of Mr. Hyde." Burns himself played Dr. Jekyll and his alter ego on an outdoor stage in the backyard. During the short skit, he underwent a complete transformation in full view of the audience by employing an old stage trick that had been effectively used for the earliest theatrical versions of the Robert Louis Stevenson story and later adapted for the 1931 Rouben Mamoulian film that won Fredric March an Oscar. The illusion was as remarkably simple as it was hair-raising. Burns already had the Mr. Hyde makeup applied in red greasepaint that was invisible under rosy stage lighting. But after he drank his potion, a blue light was gradually brought up, rendering the ghastly makeup progressively more visible. It worked – almost too well. "We scared one lady literally out of her shoes. We kept them for a couple of years, but she never came back for them."

Burns had enthusiastic assistance from many established and up-and-coming people in the special effects and makeup industries, notably Dennis Muren, presently senior effects supervisor for Industrial Light and Magic and Rick Baker, now a legendary, Academy Award-winning makeup artist. In addition to haunting his own house, Burns was keeping busy in television and theme-park shows as Kogar the Gorilla, a character he based on simian-suited stuntmen from his favorite movie serials. Rick Baker joined him, in his own gorilla suit, for the 1972 Halloween installation, "Kogar Escapes," and they scared the visitors in shifts.

Following a 1973 excursion to *Forbidden Planet* (with a detailed re-creation of Robbie the Robot constructed by Bill Malone, now an accomplished film director), Burns and company pulled out all the scare stops with a 1974 homage to *The Exorcist* called "The Thing in the Attic." Rick Baker had assisted makeup wizard Dick Smith on the film, and lent a hand for the Halloween tribute. To achieve the effect of a possessed girl's levitation, a cantilevered device that worked like a teeter-totter was installed behind a bed on a raked stage. Both

Kathy Burns and Baker's then-wife took turns in Linda Blair-inspired makeup, seemingly floating four feet above the bed, their trailing nightgowns completely hiding the trick's mechanism from view. The illusion stopped short of the film's infamous projectile bile ("We didn't want to carry it that far," says Burns), but miniature red lightbulbs embedded in the makeup caused the women's eyes to glow in a lurid, crowd-pleasing fashion. The playlet concluded with the possessed girl conjuring up a demon – Rick Baker in a scaly suit – who advanced threateningly on the audience just in time for a scream-inducing blackout.

By 1975 Bob Burns was an established neighborhood institution. Despite the crowds and increasingly bizarre spectacles (which, in addition to drawing pedestrians, managed to stop automobile traffic for blocks as gawking drivers tried to figure out just what in hell was going on), he had managed to maintain the goodwill of both nearby residents and the Burbank police department. Neighbors on either side were always willing to help out – Burns likens the local camaraderie engendered by his Halloween preparations to that attending a traditional American barn raising. Burns always held a special preview of his latest offering just for the neighbors. Only a few proved difficult. One neighbor across the street complained to the police that he was having more spillover trick-or-treaters than he could possibly handle. The police just told him to turn his lights out.

Liability insurance was, amazingly, a nonissue for people like Burns in the sixties and seventies. "We never even thought about that," recalls Burns. "People would stumble and fall, it just happened. Today, you'd get sued immediately."

In 1975, Burns staged his own miniversion of the Orson Welles *War of the Worlds* Halloween radio broadcast that had scared the bejeezus out of half the country in 1938. Welles, of course, only verbally described the invasion of the eastern seaboard by meteorlike capsules of Martians. Burns had to actually show it, and this time there was a certain amount of dissent from the neighbors. Previous shows were outrageously cute, but this time he was building a thirty-foot spacecraft, apparently smashed into his home, with all the destruction lovingly and realistically depicted. What about adjoining property values? Ever diplomatic, Burns quelled the complaints, and instead of a disaster, gave the neighborhood another nostalgic trip into retro sci-fi.

The final events were mounted in 1979 and 1982, with tributes to the films *Alien* and *Creature from the Black Lagoon*. These were the most elaborate shows of all, this time constructed as full walk-through environments that required formal approval from the Burbank fire department. They were also the biggest crowd pleasers. Actor Walter Koenig (Navigator Chekhov from *Star Trek*) lent star presence to the *Alien* installation, which utilized original props from the film, courtesy of 20th Century-Fox. The studio let Burns keep the items for his collection afterwards. The *Creature* extravaganza took Halloween celebrants into the gill man's cave, illuminated by a guide carrying a Coleman lantern. This time the fire department expressed some real concern.

"Oh, Bob," the inspector said, "for the first time we've run into a problem. You can't have a live flame." So Burns blew out the lantern. A few seconds later, one of the firemen said, "Wait a minute, you can't blow out a Coleman lantern!" He had been taken in by the flickering but completely electrical prop lamp, and by Burns's play acting. Like everything about Bob's Halloween shows, the devil was always delightfully in the details.

It should come as no surprise that Bob Burns is a living legend among Halloween enthusiasts. His health and logistics permitting (including the now-unavoidable issues of liability insurance), he is planning a comeback extravaganza, this one based on the 1951 film *The Thing from Another World*, in which James Arness played a looming extraterrestrial terrorizing an arctic outpost. Although his home displays are among the most elaborate productions of their kind, Burns nonetheless falls into a special category of Halloween entrepreneur – the "yard haunter."

Rochelle Santopoalo, founder of the Global Halloween Alliance, Inc., and editor of its magazine, *Happy Halloween*, has spent more than a decade studying the phenomenon of yard haunters, who now exist in countless numbers across the country. In their hands, the traditional jack-o'-lantern on the porch has mushroomed into a fascinating folk art movement that can include everything from macabre variations on Christmas window displays to the complete transformation of one's house and property into a fanciful approximation of the Munsters' mansion.

A baby boomer, Santopoalo grew up in Waukegan, Illinois. Her first memory of the holiday was at the age of eleven, when she was given a school assignment to write an essay on the history of Halloween. "So I went to our local bookmobile, which was two blocks away from my house, and I went in there and, lo and behold, they had this book on Halloween. I thought I had found the treasures of the world." Years later, as a doctoral candidate researching the social dynamics of Halloween for her dissertation, she experienced a distinct sense of déjà vu. "I remember looking at some of the books on artistry related to Halloween and having that same experience I had when I was eleven years old, and thinking, oh my – I have discovered this *secret.*"

Santopoalo's interest in Halloween was reawakened as an adult in 1986, when she realized that for most of the neighborhood kids, Halloween "had deteriorated into just a candy holiday. I thought, There's no fun in that." She began decorating her front yard, putting on costumes that rivaled the kids', and soon became a local institution – the "Halloween Lady."

Her academic field was health-care research, and her advisor initially pooh-poohed her eccentric choice of topic, but he warmed to the idea when she proposed approaching the subject from the theoretical framework of adult play. "As I traveled around the country and talked with people who did these elaborate displays I found they were just as intrigued with the idea that *other* people did what they did because they had no awareness of anybody else doing it. Usually they were very unusual in their community. They were basically one of a kind. The fact that I had found other people around the country was just amazing for them."

In Santopoalo's observation, the first and foremost appeal of yard haunting is the simple pleasure of creating, masterminding, and inhabiting a fantasy world, and the exhilarating freedom to do things (and be things) not permissible at any other time of the year.

Additionally, yard haunters attained local celebrity status. "In fact, some people became almost the victims of their own success. Once they started, it was hard for them to not keep doing it."

Thirdly, yard haunting seemed to reclaim a sense of community, a lost or weakened connection to the outside world. "People would come year after year to this one house – they were like beacons. Because of the stability of that particular recurring event there was an instant sense of camaraderie. They're putting out a welcome sign – they're saying, 'We're open. We want you to come.'" Since people usually have to wait in lines for haunted houses, conversation is inevitable. The result is a unique sense of social participation that Santopoalo likens to block parties.

She cites Bob Burns's celebrations as a perfect example of the kind of special bonding that Halloween can provide. "When I was out in Los Angeles about a year and a half ago, I was at somebody's Halloween party, and I mentioned that I had just gotten done visiting with Bob. One of the people at the party was just electrified – 'I remember him as a kid!' And then somebody else remembered going to his yard as a kid also. There was an instant sense of connectedness because they remembered the same house, they remembered waiting in line, they remembered going through his backyard." Such moments of active engagement are becoming rare in an increasingly virtual/voyeuristic society. "Our sense of community is not geographic any more," she says. "We have community in cyberspace, through the chat rooms and that kind of thing, but often, people don't even know their neighbors."

Of course, not everybody necessarily wants to know their neighbors, or even get along with them, and there are many examples of yard haunts that have created quite the opposite of community goodwill. Beginning in 1991, a pair of Des Plaines, Illinois, home owners mounted three years of increasingly assertive Halloween displays on their lawn. By 1994, the installation included an eight-foot-tall guillotine, a blood fountain, gravestones, coffins, and forty life-sized monsters. Angelo and Julianne Jackson-Vasos claimed to have spent fifteen thousand dollars on the spectacle, a free exhibit which drew hundreds of cars for drive-by delectation. But a neighbor's formal complaint to the city closed down the horror show with the finality of a mausoleum door clanging shut. As the *Chicago Tribune* reported, "Neighborhood battles over Christmas lights have become more common as people mount ever more elaborate displays. Now, add Halloween to the list of holidays where exuberant decoration can hit a neighborhood like a plastic cleaver on a rubber hand."

"It broke our hearts," Mrs. Jackson-Vasos told the *Tribune.* "We'd been building monsters since July. We had to throw most of it away." To add insult to injury, a tombstone-like sign the couple erected on their lawn to explain the missing display to expected hoards of visitors was also ordered removed by the police, who cited an ordinance prohibiting lawn signs. "We were just trying to do something fun for the neighborhood, and this is what we get in return," said Mrs. Jackson-Vasos, who told the paper that she and her husband were even considering moving. "But we'll still find a way to get into the spirit of things somewhere else in the near future."

France is not the most obvious place to locate images of American yard and house haunters, but as it happens, the world's foremost visual documentarian of the phenomenon lives in Paris. Artist/ photographer/filmmaker Cameron Jamie was born in Northridge, California, in 1969, and lived and worked there until the 1994 earthquake completely destroyed his home and studio. He used the disaster as an opportunity to relocate to Europe, where his explorations of suburbia's dark side have garnered him many gallery exhibits, much critical praise, and a residency in Paris — not to mention outright incredulity from people who often think his stark, black-and-white photos of San Fernando Valley tract houses made over as mausoleums are Jamie's fabrications, and not found imagery.

Since the 1980s, Jamie has been photographing a kind of Halloween house quite different from Bob Burns's nostalgic Hollywood tributes, or the neighborhood-friendly haunts so lovingly chronicled by *Happy Halloween* magazine. These are small-scale, often very downscale installations, sometimes truly family affairs, often not well publicized or even well visited. Jamie likens them to professional wrestling (another of his documentary interests) as an outlet for the stifled theatrical impulses of the lower middle class. "You don't generally see spook houses in central metropolitan areas. They're always exiled to the suburbs," he says.

A large percentage of his work documents haunted houses in the San Fernando Valley, where he believes the proximity of the motion-picture industry predisposes ordinary people to role-playing and fantasy. He returns to the States every October to continue his singular exploration. Over the years, he has captured thousands of images, many of them disturbing and weirdly poignant. Indeed, his photographs evoke territory previously explored by Diane Arbus, with perhaps just a whiff of John Waters. People transform their kitchens into places of human sacrifice, their bedrooms into crematoriums. Tidy homes become disaster areas. Graves are dug in front yards, the dirt piled up. "The haunted house is a dirty house," Jamie says. "Once a year Halloween allows people to turn their house into a Dumpster. Halloween and horror movies are basically about the American fear of dirt and disorder."

Just as *The Munsters* and *The Addams Family* parodied middle-class behavior standards, so, too, do these homegrown Halloween productions allow a spontaneous ritual skewering of suburban values. Odd psychodramas unfold as parents and children enact roles of victims and victimizers. Jamie vividly describes one house he visited, in which a mad-scientist mother performed crude "plastic surgery" on her teenage son, all the while cackling, "Now you'll be exactly what I've always wanted!" Family members are replaced by effigies of witches and aliens in their favorite TV chairs, while crummy monster movies unreel monotonously on the VCR. Ovens, appliances, even toilets are reconfigured as devouring maws. Undercurrents of domestic violence and family dysfunction bubble up everywhere as the American dream is transmogrified into a hellish trap, lit by flickering candles, strobe lights, and lava lamps.

As grassroots Halloween enthusiasm began percolating throughout America in the 1970s and 1980s, commercial theme parks began to experiment with October haunts. Knott's Berry Farm was the first, and its annual "Knott's Scary Farm" attraction is still going strong thirty years later. Many observers credit the Halloween gambit with saving the park financially. Over several seasons in the 1970s, Knott's perfected its formula – atmospherically re-dressing the park for evening visitors, with added walk-through mazes – which has since been imitated by scores of amusement parks across the country hungry for off-season income. But in sheer numbers, homegrown haunts sponsored by local nonprofit agencies probably had more to do with Halloween's steady ascent in popularity.

Leonard Pickel is the editor of *Haunted Attraction*, a trade magazine based in Myrtle Beach, South Carolina. Both a journalist and hands-on design consultant, he is probably the world's foremost authority on the dark amusement industry. A late baby boomer, Pickel remembers being impressed by a Jaycees haunted house in Dallas when he was still in high school. "It would be a provocative concept even today," he recalls. "The whole haunted house was completely pitch black – you couldn't see your hand in front of your face." Periodically, a strobe light would come on, illuminating actors in ghoulish getups. "Then the strobe would go off, leaving you in the dark with the monsters again. That had quite an effect on me. Some teenage girls who were friends were absolutely terrified. It was a very effective show."

At that time, Pickel had never even considered haunting as a career choice. He was interested in architecture, and went on to earn a degree at Texas A&M University. There, as a freshman, Halloween provided him with a school-sanctioned way to meet girls. "The residence association had set up a deal where, for one hour, the guys could go over to the girls' dorms and trick-or-treat. Then, for the next hour, the girls would visit the guys." Since outrageous male plumage has always been been part of the mating ritual, in both the human and animal worlds, Pickel and his roommate dressed up. "He went as Groucho Marx, and I threw together a Dracula costume from a cape that I had and a white shirt. We cut the point off of a beat-up wooden stake and attached that to a belt and put that under my shirt, so I was Dracula with a stake in my heart." The gambit worked, and some of the girls even invited them in. "Now it was our turn," Pickel recalls. "We came running back to our dorm room, trying to throw together some decorations." The roommate had a portrait of his great-grandfather, painted by his own mother. "The face was kind of weak," says Pickel. Heirloom considerations notwithstanding, "Just messing around, we painted over a werewolf face." They placed a candle in front of the painting and put a red lightbulb in their room lamp. Pickel laid himself out on a coffee table, his stake sticking up. Groucho sat in a chair, twiddling his cigar. The same candy they had collected from the girls' dorm was placed in a bowl on the far side of the bier. "Our concept was to make the girls come in, reach over Dracula to get the candy, and then I would grab them."

However, "it didn't dawn on us that the girls were going over to the more expensive, air-conditioned dorms, and the jock dorms, and they weren't necessarily coming over in droves to the low-rent freshman dorm," says Pickel. "But eventually, we did hear some knock-knock-knock giggle-giggle-giggle and 'trick or treat' from down the hallway. As they got to our door, I can remember seeing three heads kind of peering into the open doorway, and the fourth girl walked straight in, but she only got about two or three steps, and just screamed. And we never saw them again. My roommate and I looked at each other at the same time and said, if they were *that* easy to scare, we've got to do a haunted house."

The following year, they made a proposal to their dorm council and received approval for a haunted house in the dorm's basement, budgeted at around three hundred dollars. "We used the game area, TV area, and a couple of the hallways, and begged, borrowed, and stole props, masks, and jam boxes – they weren't even called that back then, but that's what they were, little tape players with speakers. I think we were charging fifty cents a head. We were open for two nights and were hoping there might be enough money left over to throw a party or something for the dorm." To everyone's amazement, "When we were done, we had grossed one thousand dollars."

Repeat business helped. "There were guys that were going over to the girls' dorms and picking up a girl and bringing her over. For a buck, the two of them would go through the haunted house, and she would grope him all the way through. Then he'd take her back, get another girl, and come back for another dollar. By the time he was done, he'd had the time of his life for ten bucks."

After graduation, while apprenticing in Dallas-area architectural firms, Pickel heard about a March of Dimes haunted house and offered his services as a volunteer. Near the end of the first meeting he attended, just as everyone was getting ready to leave, he raised some eyebrows by telling the steering committee, "I think all of your room designs are backward." Asked to explain himself, he pointed out that each of the proposed "scares" was immediately in the face of the first person to enter the room. "If you do that, you're going to bottleneck these people to the point that you won't be able to push any kind of large numbers through the attraction." People started to take their coats off and listen. They took some of his advice, ended up having a record season, and the following year asked Pickel himself to serve as the committee chairman.

His architectural training, of course, proved extremely useful, though in a perversely counterintuitive way. "In architecture school they teach you how to shape a room in order to make people comfortable," he says. Here, the goal was exactly the opposite. Discomfort and disorientation were the guiding principles. Previously, the March of Dimes had been building its haunted house on a four-foot grid pattern – basically, because plywood was manufactured in a standard four-foot width. The result was a square, static floor plan with wasted space. "I'm not sure how I made the leap, but it made more sense to me to narrow up those corridors on a triangular grid." Triangular structures are also inherently stronger, and don't require a lot of extra bracing. The resulting claustrophobic hairpin turns proved a much more efficient use of interior space, and, by increasing the overall length of the walkway, accommodated more people, and raised all that much more money.

Pickel chaired the Dallas March of Dimes house for four years in the 1980s, but he sensed that the era of the nonprofit haunt was coming to an end. Still, charity-based charnel houses were crucially important to the exponential growth of Halloween as a modern national obsession. The Jaycees claim responsibility for instituting the first scary fund-raiser, though there is some controversy over exactly which city hosted it. A 1971 Jaycees haunted house in Philadelphia was so successful that the chapter published a how-to handbook that went to every Jaycees organization in the country. "Overnight," says Pickel, "it went from having a few seasonal haunted houses to having hundreds, then thousands. Then other charities jumped on the bandwagon. There were several charity haunts around the country that just started doing huge numbers and it wasn't long before the entrepreneurial element noticed, and started contracting with charities for a percentage of the gross, or just doing it themselves."

Tired of the March of Dimes volunteer gig, with its budgetary restrictions that occasionally found him "pulling money out of my own pocket for a cool prop or light-beam effect," Pickel became an entrepreneur himself. He called his business "Halloween Haun-trepreneurs."

"Slowly but surely, in almost all markets, the for-profit haunted houses pushed the nonprofit haunted houses out of business, either to extinction or to a much more limited role," he says. It will startle no one to learn that the main reason was money. "A for-profit haunted house can spend five thousand dollars on a prop, it can spend one hundred thousand dollars on advertising if it wants to. A nonprofit event just can't compete with that kind of capital." There are a few notable exceptions, and Pickel notes the Hangman's

Haunted House in Fort Worth and the Rocky Point Haunted House in Salt Lake City as extremely well run nonprofit ventures.

Among Pickel's Hauntrepreneurial activities were Mayhem Manor, a year-round haunted house in Myrtle Beach that he ran for seven years; consulting work with major theme parks; and, finally, the venue through which his public knows him best, *Haunted Attraction*. Founded as an eight-page newsletter in 1994, the publication has now evolved into a glossy quarterly magazine.

*Haunted Attraction* has all the features of a typical trade publication: profiles of successful businesspeople and their flourishing ventures, news about conventions and conferences, advertisements for new products and services, all presented in the gung-ho cadences of motivational zeal. But the prize at the end of *Haunted Attraction*'s dark rainbow is less a treasure chest than a burial vault. The usual trappings and indicators of American success – material splendor, physical beauty, and health – are turned on their decapitated heads. Viewed through the omnipresent prism of Halloween, the most valuable houses in *Haunted Attraction* are the most spectacularly delapidated, and the most desirable bodies are those in advanced stages of decomposition, or at least grievously wounded. In place of the homey chic of Restoration Hardware, the advertisements have an aesthetic all their own, which might be dubbed Resurrection Hardcore. DO YOUR CREATURES SEEM A LITTLE DEAD? asks an ad for Effective Engineering in San Diego. If so, an animatronic decoder will restore your get-up-and-gore. Many mainstream businesses employ slogans along the lines of TAKE A BITE OUT OF YOUR COMPETITION, but Stage Fright Studios of Kansas City means it literally. Terror Wear specializes in haunted-house T-shirts. A recurring page, designed along the lines of a Friday the thirteenth real estate section, offers full haunted-house environments for resale, complete with interior walls and façades, fog machines, air compressors, smoke detectors, and emergency lights. If you have the need, $125,000 can buy you a pair of walk-through haunts, their interior props including "Fireplace, Piano, Living Wall, Dancing Ghost, Canopy Bed with Body, Storm Window, Kitchen Cabinet, Stove, Refrigerator, Meat Locker, Dining Table with Chairs, Metal Cage, Boiler and Pipes, Lab Tables and Bodies, 8-foot Mechanical Spider, Sacrifice Table with Body, Volcano, and Pneumatic Devil." In short, all the comforts of home. But is owning two haunted houses just conspicuous consumption? No, says Pickel, explaining that one of the strongest trends in the Halloween business are installations involving multiple individual attractions, which simultaneously increases capacity and dramatically increases the potential admission price.

Like shelter magazines, *Haunted Attraction* regularly includes how-to articles, with an emphasis on cost-saving approaches to building things like Victorian house fronts and crackling electric chairs, as well as nuts-and-bolts tips on budgeting and promotion. Pickel hosts or participates in several workshops or trade shows each year; the largest is the Transworld Halloween Costume and Party Show, which brings hundreds of vendors together in Chicago each year to share information and innovations.

Fire marshals and safety codes are an issue of common concern in the haunted-attraction business – and a problem taken far more seriously after a 1987 haunted-house fire at Great Adventure amusement park in New Jersey, in which eight young people were killed. "Before that, haunted houses kind of fell through the cracks," Pickel says. The Great Adventure tragedy occurred in a maze that looped through six semi-trailers. When a malfunctioning strobe light left part of the attraction in pitch blackness, a kid decided to light his way with a cigarette lighter, and promptly collided with foam rubber wall padding – ironically intended as a safety feature. Foam rubber is highly flammable, and with no emergency exits, all directions in the zigzagging labyrinth led fatally back to smoke and flames. The young man who set the fire escaped early and, afraid he'd be in trouble, didn't call for help. The incident received heavy nationwide media coverage, and codes were upgraded across the country. While specific requirements can vary almost capriciously from municipality to municipality, explains Pickel, the ground rules are uniform, including "a mandatory sprinkler system, nonflamm-ability of walls and everything, and of course, smoke detection, which is what really saves lives. Fire doesn't really kill people, it's smoke inhalation."

So, beyond the safety precautions, what are Leonard Pickel's secrets for operating a surefire haunted house? "If you're looking for a business, a haunted house is just like running any other business," he says. "You have to watch your costs, you have to advertise well, and you have to have a decent show – you don't have to have a great show, but you have to have a *decent* show. The public wants to be scared. They're looking for that adrenaline rush, they want you to scare them, and if you don't, they're going to be mad." Of course, what horrifies one person might just send someone else into a laughing fit. "There's a certain percentage of the population that's going to scream at anything," Pickel admits, "and others who could be locked in a coffin and physically buried without being scared." But, whatever the challenges, "people who are going to a haunted house in October are looking, literally, to have the bladder scared out of them."[10]

While Pickel is a an expert on state-of-the-art scares, and can authoritatively advise you on the most technologically advanced methods to make a skeleton dance or a zombie rot, he also finds that some of the most effective scream producers are accomplished with

10. Though not widely discussed, haunted attractions and thrill rides have always had to deal with episodes of urinary incontinence. If someone pees on the Haunted Mansion ride at Disneyland, a worker is directed to board the "doombuggy" and mop up the mess while patrons on either side continue to enjoy the haunt, blissfully unaware of anyone else's embarrassment.

minimal investment of money and materials. Take, for example, the story of Pickel and the giant rat. He had conceived a supreme horror effect for one of his haunts: a rat head the size of a Volkswagen that would come crashing through a doorway. "My mother happened to be in town and overheard me talking about it," he recalls. "And the next morning I had this eighteen-inch, very cute gray mouse head she had made out of fur, with a little black nose and some ears." It wasn't scary, and obviously wasn't as big as he had envisioned it. But it was his mom's home handiwork, and Pickel went ahead and installed it in the haunted house. He cut a hole about the size of a doghouse door into the wall, and had a puppeteer just shove it out as people walked by. "You could see people jump past the hole because they didn't know what was going to come out of it. And when it did, they'd yell. I was walking through the hall one night when I heard this continuous, bloodcurdling scream. I thought, maybe someone got seriously hurt. I ran around the corner and found this girl in a fetal position over in the corner, and this other young girl who was working the rat, with her full arm extended through the rat hole. It was obvious it wasn't a real rat, you could see her arm and everything, but the other girl was just in hysterics, terrified of this giant rat." Pickel took the puppeteer aside and tried to explain that the purpose of the rat was to keep people moving down the hall, not to stop the show.

"Scaring people is like telling a joke," says Pickel. "It's all in the timing. And changing some minor thing can change everything." He describes the lesson he learned trying to "improve" the rat trick. He added a laboratory and an expository back story about experimenting on rodents, the experiment du jour involving mysterious growth hormones. "I decorated up the laboratory, made it look really cool, with a lot of stuff to see, a lot of eye candy – and completely destroyed the scare factor. Because now people were coming into the room and looking at all the cool stuff, and they never saw the rat." Pickel stripped out the props and restored his original, minimalist concept.

It worked. And, once again, the sweet music of screams was heard across the land.

David Lady was born on Halloween. So was his mother. Forty years after David's birth, they still celebrate the holiday together, and she never fails to dress up like a witch. Mrs. Lady is the official ticket taker at the Horror Hotel Monster Museum in Chatfield, Ohio, a popular seasonal attraction run by her son for the last nine years. A former railroad hotel built in the middle of the nineteenth century on the well-traveled run between Columbus and Sandusky, Horror Hotel is also the year-round home of David and his wife, Laura, who shares his lifelong fascination with all things fun and spooky.

Although the railroad is long gone, Sandusky Avenue in Chatfield, also known as Ohio Route 4, is still a major truck artery at all hours, which makes traditional trick-or-treating a risky proposition for local youngsters.

"They let them close it off every Halloween and do a parade while angry semi drivers sit and blow their car horns and curse the day that we all were born," Lady says. "The kids parade through town in their costumes, with high school bands, little business floats, politicians sitting on tops of convertibles, stuff like that. They go around the town, and it ends up at the elementary school, where everybody, the kids all get a treat bag, because being such a heavily trafficked road, they can't really have trick-or-treat proper. It was just deemed too unsafe for that."

Contained attractions like Horror Hotel also fill in the trick-or-treat void. Unlike many Halloween exhibits, Horror Hotel cultivates a family audience and avoids startling effects and an excess of gore. Basically, Horror Hotel answers the burning question: when movie monsters go on their Halloween vacations, where do they stay? "Halloween is the time of year when all the monsters and ghosts and strange creatures materialize on earth, in the land of the living, and we provide accommodations for them," Lady explains. "So we have monster maids, housekeepers, bellhops, cooks, desk clerks, and the guy from *Tomb of the Blind Dead* is usually the desk clerk."

The two-story, ten-bedroom mansion features full-scale replicas (or at least lovingly re-created masks) of just about every film fiend that ever was, in elaborate, tongue-in-cheek dioramas visited by as many as a hundred pilgrims per night every weekend in October. Many are loyal returnees, and not a few kids and adults recognize Lady's mother from her real-life job running the cafeteria at the middle school in nearby Bucyrus – a post she's held for thirty-two years.

Growing up a Halloween baby, David had the added treat of his birthday being celebrated by just about everybody in Bucyrus, Ohio, even people who didn't know him. The stores were full of skeletons and pumpkins and witches. Naturally, he felt proprietary about Halloween and its accoutrements. More than a mere accident of birth, Halloween was also something of an entitlement. He began amassing creepy collectibles quite early on.

"One of the first things I remember owning was a poster of Bela Lugosi as Dracula. I remember that my grandmother hated it and was afraid of it, so I liked it even more."

His mother was more sympathetic. "If I would look in *TV Guide* and there would be a Lugosi or Karloff movie on at three A.M. – this was before VCRs – Mom would get me up. Mom would set her alarm clock and say, 'David? You want to come downstairs? Your Lugosi movie's on.' And she would let me go down in my pajamas and watch the horror movie. Sometimes she would bring me toast and hot chocolate and stuff and sit there and watch some of it with me. Occasionally, my dad would wander in and angrily grumble,

'Christ! This is a fine thing to be watching late at night! You won't get any damn sleep!' Dad didn't relate too well to the whole monster thing, and thought I was weird. I know I was a disappointment to him for a long time, and wasn't into any of the things that he was into – sports, cars, things like that. I was the town freak, there's no doubt."

Like most monster fans of his generation, Lady was weaned on Forrest J. Ackerman's legendary magazine *Famous Monsters of Filmland*, a funny, punny, bimonthly paean to Hollywood's cobwebby pantheon that inspired some of the horror field's heaviest hitters, including Stephen King and Academy Award-winning makeup artist Rick Baker. The wisecracking spirit of the magazine seems to infect every inch of Horror Hotel – take, for instance, the mad scientist's laboratory filled with animated, cackling "Jekyll Lanterns."

*Famous Monsters* was almost like having Halloween every eight weeks instead of just once a year. According to Lady, "the high point of each new issue wasn't so much the movie plot synopses or even the awesome stills, but a little section at the back of the magazine from which one could order from an outfit called the Captain Company just about everything necessary for a perfect life." Everything included realistic rubber spiders, life-size posters of Dracula and Frankenstein, skull mugs, miniature guillotines, but most of all, meticulously fabricated latex monster masks from Don Post Studios in California. The Post company was the first manufacturer to license the Universal Studios monster characters, beginning with a rubber Frankenstein mask in 1948 that coincided with the release of the popular horror comedy *Abbott and Costello Meet Frankenstein*. Post had started his business during World War II with novelty masks of dictators like Hitler, Mussolini, and Stalin. But Post's real fortune was to be made in monsters. By the 1960s, an entire line of Don Post Universal Studios monster masks were available. Unlike the run-of-the-mill Halloween masks, usually made of rigid plastic, the Post product had unprecedented flexibility and detailing, not to mention hair.

"Many of us spent hours staring at those mask photos, picking our favorites, and wondering how on earth we'd ever talk our parents into shelling out thirty-five bucks for something to make us look hideous," recalled Lady. His first Post mask was the Creature from the Black Lagoon. "I took him to school with me, drew sketches of him, snapped photos of him peeking from behind trees in the backyard, and always returned him to his place of honor at night – on the nightstand next to my bed, where the single green Christmas light I'd placed inside him provided me with the only Creature-head night-light on the block."

Some youthful *Famous Monsters* devotees, like Steven Spielberg, were inspired to produce their own eight-millimeter experiments in shock, but David Lady was fascinated with with spook houses. "I'd tear up the garage every year," he says. He didn't have much to fabricate his Halloween walk-through mazes from, aside from recycled cardboard, some masks, and his imagination, but he attracted a following of neighborhood kids nonetheless. When an emergency rose, Mom was always there. When one of David's friends got sick, "she had to lay in a coffin in the garage with a mask," and never complained.

He traces his particular obsession with walk-through horror environments to family vacations. "We used to take vacations and we went to places like Myrtle Beach and Niagara Falls, especially the Canadian side where they have a lot of wax museums and haunted old fun houses and mazes. I loved to go through that stuff." Another indelible impression was made by the Haunted Mansion at Disneyland and Disney World. "I saw it in Florida first," he remembers. "My mom loves Florida because it's unbearably hot there, so every summer, during the hottest time of year we would go to Florida and would sweat like chunks of rancid pork. I don't know why we didn't go in March or something sensible, but every summer we went to Florida. But anyplace where there was a wax museum, or a spook house, or a fun house or anything, I would whine and beg until I would get taken."

Lady's haunted houses became increasingly ambitious during his high school years. One returning guest was his wife-to-be, Laura. "Eventually she ended up helping at one of them because I was an idiot high school guy and all my friends were idiot high school guys and we always needed more help. So we put her in like a torn-up, tie-dyed bedsheet and a rubber mask and she hid in the maze to scare people." By this time Lady had patched things up with his father, who became one of his staunchest supporters and unofficial public relations spokesman.

After graduating high school in 1980, Laura and David spent more time together, not all of it involving haunted houses. (He confides that their first kiss transpired through the latex barrier of a monster mask.) Eventually it occurred to them that any real work involving masks and monsters was likely to be located somewhere other than Bucyrus. They were married in 1985 and moved to Los Angeles. By this time Lady had become an accomplished sculptor and mask maker in his own right. However, movie-related work in L.A. just didn't take off. "I did some movie work out there. I played about six different zombies in the timeless classic *Zombiethon* – a wonderful film that you can really be proud to show your mother – a combination of naked women and gore effects. It was fun. I'm not sorry I did it; I'm glad I did it; if anybody comes to me now and says, 'Be in my cheap, stupid, awful, low-budget movie,' I'm there, with whatever they want."

Meanwhile, the Ladys managed to establish a thriving mail-order business, fabricating and customizing monster masks for fans and collectors all across the country. "We do it all – molding, sculpting, casting, painting, hairing" as well as improving and restyling existing masks. "If you buy something mass produced, it's generally not done with the greatest detail work, so people send it to us and say, "Can you repaint this so it looks more accurately like the one in the movie? Can you add more hair?"

As the mask business became more profitable, the couple realized that "we weren't really making much income off the fact that we were living in Hollywood. We were making income through mail order, which you can do from anywhere." They had long considered leaving Los Angeles, and the 1992 riots following the Rodney King verdict amounted to the deciding straw.

"We came back here and said we wanted a big, dark, drafty, spooky old house and all the Realtors thought we were kidding." The real estate people kept pushing bright little starter homes. " 'Oh, here's nice place for a young couple, here's a cute little ranch-style.' And we were like, 'No, if we want cute, we'll buy a teddy bear.'" The Ladys, of course, really wanted room for werewolves. "Do you plan to have children?" the Realtors asked, curious about their need for so much space. "Why do you need all that room?" they asked. "Because we . . . make things," came their cryptic answer.

Finally, a Realtor in Bucyrus called. "You said you wanted a big, old, spooky-looking place. How about the old hotel out in Chatfield?" Both David and Laura had driven by the location "a million times" en route to the legendary Sandusky amusement park Cedar Point, but never noticed the property.

"It was offered for sale by a little old lady who lived here all alone and only lived in three rooms," Lady recalls. The rest of the building was a mess. "There was incredible dust, filth, and the ceilings were drooping and the wallpaper was peeling. So, of course we needed to buy it."

Lady admits that the building "needed some fixing up even by haunted-house people's standards," but at sixty-five thousand dollars the old hotel was a steal. And the mortgage ended up costing less per month than their "itty-bitty" apartment in the Ukrainian district of West Hollywood. "We didn't even move here with the intention of opening it up to the public as Horror Hotel. I have a newspaper article from when we moved here, a 'Look! Weirdos move to town!' kind of story. And they quoted me as saying, no, we're not going to open it up to the public because it's our home."

But being back in their old haunting grounds rapidly generated nostalgia for the haunted houses they had previously created in Bucyrus. "We were depressed because we didn't have a Halloween project and we thought, well, gosh . . . and suddenly it occurred to us, we live in what looks like a haunted house anyway. Why don't we just take people through?"

Their previous efforts, however, "were mostly attended by rowdy teenagers who wanted to show off their machismo – and some of the male teenagers were even worse." A compromise was struck. "We tried to make it kind of a cross between a haunted house and a wax museum. Less violent and threatening than a haunted house, but a little more interactive than a wax museum. So it's somewhere in between."

The first year was a tentative experiment. "We didn't know if anyone would want to come or not, so everything was very cheap and done very raggedly, with things made out of cardboard and duct tape." To Lady's amazement, people came. "The rowdy teenagers who just wanted to grope their girlfriends in a dark maze were disappointed, but the people who aren't too keen on being really terrorized and having their kids traumatized loved us for it, and every year we've had a better and better and more responsive and receptive audience."

Over the next eight Octobers, Horror Hotel evolved its present, crowd-pleasing format. The Ladys stop taking orders for masks and display heads in late July, and spend every August and September preparing for their own Halloween season in Chatfield. "We usually have somewhere in the neighborhood of fifty or sixty life-size figures standing around in various poses." Laura Lady is responsible for costuming, as well as wigs and hair ("I call her my 'head of hair,'" says her husband, with a typical arching of one eyebrow).

The Ladys personally escort small groups of visitors, who pay five dollars a head, through their domain. They are accompanied by yet another "head" – a talking skull in a box, who delivers most of the evening's bon mots. The skull box contains a concealed cassette player, which delivers a narration prerecorded by Burbank-based actor Daniel Roebuck, himself a major fan of the horror genre. Roebuck's plummy diction "is kind of a cross between Boris Karloff and Hans Conried," according to Lady.

"I always write the script for what's going to be in each scene and then I fax it to him, and then we usually have a couple phone calls where he says, 'What am I seeing here?' and we kind of go over how the skull is thinking, whether the skull is alarmed or thinks it's funny, or whatever, and then he sends me back a tape. It's all timed with how many seconds each thing needs to run, and he always does it magnificently."

The visitors encounter the talking skull on the entryway table. "The skull welcomes the guests," says Lady, "and then asks for my help. 'If my associate here would be so good as to carry me through . . .' because, of course, he's only a skull. That gives me an excuse to carry him around. People look at the skull because he's doing the talking, and his mouth is moving, and so when I want you to look in a certain area, the skull says, 'Oh, my, over there I see we have . . .' and I just aim him like this and it's amazing – people don't look at me as much as they just follow the skull."

During the tour, visitors view not only the Ladys' masks but full monster bodies as well, elaborately costumed by Laura. Although a percentage of the forms are recycled/re-dressed store mannequins, others have to be made from the ground up, from skeletal armatures fleshed out with foam rubber. Unfortunately, says Lady, "a lot of premade store mannequins are in strange, high-fashion poses. If anybody really stood like that, they'd be rushed to a chiropractor." Physical grotesquerie, apparently, has its limits, even in the realm of the monstrous.

And just who are the thousand or more souls who come to visit the Ladys each October? "We get the nicest people," David says. "We get art students and movie buffs and families with little kids who wouldn't take them to any other haunted house. I can't tell you how many times somebody has come up to me in a Wal-Mart and said, 'Hey, we came to your hotel and we loved it. It's the only one that I'll let my kids go to, because they cry when, you know, they get too scared.' So Horror Hotel kind of gives them a chance to confront all those things that they're afraid of.

"And, you know, Jason and Freddy and everybody *are* in here, but they don't attack, so the kids who are really scared of monsters have their sense of bravery reinforced when they get out and nothing bad happened. We promise at the beginning that nothing will pop out or chase you down. We don't want you to go through with your eyes closed, scared to look at anything. We want you to look because we detail it to the max."

The Ladys' reluctance to indulge in gross-outs and visceral shocks also has the unexpected benefit of attracting senior citizens. "It turns out that a lot of older people still love Halloween, but you know, when you're seventy-nine years old, you don't want to go in a place that's going to be totally dark and you're having to feel your way through, or maybe trip over something weird on the floor. These people come and bring their grandkids, and I think they enjoy it as much as anybody. They get all the jokes, and they remember

Frankenstein and Dracula and the Wolf Man from their younger days."

To maximize revenues from its brief autumn season, a visit to Horror Hotel concludes with an obligatory exit through a frighteningly well stocked gift shop, including samples of the Ladys' mask work, David's self-published guide to mask collecting, as well as plastic vampire fangs, fake blood, and other goodies. "We have Horror Hotel towels, which sell pretty good," Lady explains, "because you can convince people you stayed at a place called Horror Hotel and stole a towel." New this year is a video, *Horror Hotel: The Take-Home Experience*, as well as a CD packed with "weird music for Halloween haunted houses and parties and stuff." The disc includes "howls, screams, moans, zombie breathing, rattling chains, clanking, and spooky noises," according to Lady. "I do good zombie-breathing effects, so we have those on there. Most of the voices on it are me."

Finally, Horror Hotel always does its community payback by way of an annual Red Cross blood drive. "We usually try to have some sort of giveaway thing, if you donate blood you get either a free ticket to Horror Hotel or something. A couple of years ago we had mints made up – mints in little wrappers that said 'Horror Hotel' – you know, like when you stay in a fancy hotel and there's a mint on the pillow." The nurses put on pale makeup with two holes on their necks, and Lady, naturally, wears a vampire costume. "I always say, 'Come, donate blood. Vampires aren't the only ones who need it.' "

Clive Barker's name has become almost synonymous with the dark side of popular culture, though a visit to his sunny Beverly Hills home is quite unlike a trip to Horror Hotel. The author of the *Books of Blood* and the filmmaker who created *Hellraiser* doesn't dwell in a monster museum; rather, he lives and works in a tasteful and airy compound of three houses, one of which is completely devoted to his other creative interest, painting.

Born in 1952, Barker grew up in Liverpool, and developed a long-distance love affair with Halloween through American movies like *Meet Me in St. Louis* and the writing of Ray Bradbury. He remembers watching stateside television programs every October "and being sick with envy, wanting to be part of this American experience." Barker was keenly interested in dark rides and spook houses, but his mother was dead set against the fun fairs where they might be found. "She thought they were run by Gypsies, which they tended to be, and were therefore dangerous places. My mom has this thing about Gypsies," he explains. Later, when he lived in London, he encountered a couple of ghost rides installed at Hampstead Heath during Easter. But his own direct experience with haunted attractions was surprisingly limited when Universal Studios Hollywood asked him, based on his name-brand reputation as a king of horror, to create a walk-through event for their "Halloween Horror Nights" in 1998.

"I came into this sideways," he admits, "not knowing a lot about Halloween haunts, certainly not anything about them as an art form. It was only when I started to create them myself that I realized there were magazines about them, and that there was a whole tradition involved."

Barker had spent years writing and directing in London's fringe theater scene, producing Grand Guignolish plays like *Frankenstein in Love* (1982), and instinctively understood that haunted houses were a uniquely American hybrid of theater, painting, architecture, sculpture, and puppetry. "It's environmental," he observes. He relates the haunted house to the 1960s phenomenon of the Happening and the contemporary performance art of Julian Beck's Living Theater, "formless experiences that turned on nudity, snatches of Sophocles, a little more nudity, and then violence

∧
∧

DEATH KICKS UP ITS HEELS: A 1493 German woodcut by Michael Wolgemut.

THE CANDY MAN: Halloween poisoner Ronald Clark O'Bryan, who murdered his own son in 1974.

∨
∨

THE JACK-O'-LANTERN was traditionally carved from a turnip in Europe, but immigrants found a superior vegetable in North America. "The Pumpkin Effigy," an 1867 *Harper's Weekly* illustration by L.W. Atwater.

BRITISH CHILDREN PARADE an effigy in celebration of
Guy Fawkes Day. The November 5 holiday had a strong influence on
the development of Halloween as we know it today. Illustration from
Chambers's *The Book of Days* (1865).

THE EVOLUTION of a Halloween icon. Witch-like attire was a common feature of English country dress.

ILLUSTRATOR W.W. Denslow's festive conception of the Wicked Witch of the West, from L. Frank Baum's *The Wonderful Wizard of Oz* (1900).

THE CLASSIC Halloween witch, with broomstick and feline-familiar. Early twentieth-century illustration; artist unknown.

MARGARET O'BRIEN is initiated into the mysteries of Halloween in
Vincente Minnelli's *Meet Me in St. Louis* (1944).

BETTY GRABLE gets into the Halloween mood in this 1940s publicity photo.

GLAMOROUS stars like Joan Crawford always found time for holiday publicity opportunities.

VERONICA LAKE'S *I Married a Witch* (1942) was a perfect Halloween tie-in.

The Wonders of the Invisible World:

Being an Account of the

# TRYALS

OF

## Several Witches,

Lately Executed in

# NEW-ENGLAND:

And of several remarkable.Curiosities therein Occurring.

Together with,

I. Observations upon the Nature, the Number, and the Operations of the Devils.

II. A short Narrative of a late outrage committed by a knot of Witches in Swede-Land, very much resembling, and so far explaining, that under which New-England has laboured.

III. Some Councels directing a due Improvement of the Terrible things lately done by the unusual and amazing Range of Evil-Spirits in New-England.

IV. A brief Discourse upon those Temptations which are the more ordinary Devices of Satan.

By COTTON MATHER.

Published by the Special Command of his EXCELLENCY the Governor of the Province of the Massachusets-Bay in New-England.

Printed first, at Boston in New-England; and Reprinted at London, for John Dunton, at the Raven in the Poultry. 1693.

COTTON MATHER'S 1693
account of the Salem witch trials.

HOLIDAY REVELERS in modern Salem, which has aggressively
promoted itself as a Halloween capital.

LEGENDARY Halloween "yard haunter" Bob Burns staged some of the most elaborate home displays ever attempted at his Burbank residence. A gravity-defying homage to *The Exorcist* (1974).

"GOOMBAH," an Octopoid alien, landed on Burns's roof for Halloween 1970.

BURNS morphs into Mr. Hyde (1971).

AN AMERICAN Halloween party, circa 1920.

AN EMBOSSED 1909 postcard.

EARLY TWENTIETH-CENTURY POSTCARDS are among the most vivid repositories of traditional Halloween imagery.

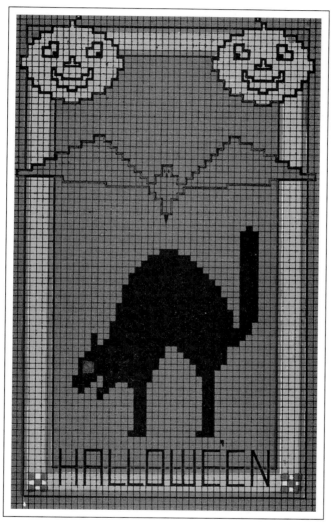

AN UNUSUAL 1919 postcard, strongly
influenced by the arts and crafts movement

∧
∧

HALLOWEEN was sometimes called "Snap-Apple Night," and revelers traditionally utilized apples and nuts in games of skill and fortune-telling. American postcard, circa 1909.

A SPOOKY Halloween prank, circa 1909, commemorated by a postcard published in both America and Europe.

∨
∨

THE GREENWICH VILLAGE Halloween Parade, a
New York institution, shown here in 1996.

SAN FRANCISCO'S Castro Street celebration, shown
here in 2001, has traditionally emphasized gender-bending.

Photofest

A POSTER for John Carpenter's *Halloween* (1978), one of the most successful and influential independent films ever made.

HOMICIDE FOR THE HOLIDAY: *Halloween*'s psycho-killer "Michael Myers" inspired a slew of slasher pictures.

Photofest

HALLOWEEN IN AMERICA treats the subject of death
indirectly, through pop culture revenants like Frankenstein's monster,
the Mummy, and Dracula, seen above at Madame Tussaud's, New York,
in October 2001. But the parallel Mexican celebration, the Day of the
Dead, involves a heartfelt acknowledgment of departed loved ones.

AP/Wide World Photos

∧
∧

AN OSAMA BIN LADEN Halloween Mask, Mexico City 2001.

SEPTEMBER 11 and October 31: A jack-o'-lantern display in Providence, Rhode Island, commemorates a national tragedy.

∨
∨

AP/Wide World Photos

and atmospheric effects. You weren't ever sure what was going to happen next."

Nudity, of course, wasn't going to happen at Halloween Horror Nights, but the Universal parks had established a reputation for providing strong meat for the October crowds who lined up to be scared in Hollywood and Orlando. This author served as a Halloween consultant to Universal Studios Florida in the early 1990s, and was frankly surprised at how grisly the holiday had become – even as I posed for wacko publicity photos, fondling a machete outside a replica of the *Psycho* house. The *Psycho* walk-through included the almost existential nonstop spectacle of a mannequin being stabbed behind a shower curtain, which ran with both cascading water and spurting blood. But perhaps the most memorable scare of the evening involved a screaming woman trapped in a coffin swarming with live rats (in reality, she was their owner/ trainer, and not at all scared). The coffin was hidden in darkness under a Plexiglas floor, and was only illuminated when you were standing, helpless, directly above the rodent-teeming grave.

"Of course, much of the imagery is crass and stupid," says Barker, "but some of it is curiously eloquent." He views the haunted house, with its grisly dummies and animatronics, as a historical extension of the puppet tradition. Punchinello, he notes, "was an incredibly violent fellow who killed without remorse – a serial killer, really. He kills his wife, he throws the baby out the window, while Toby the dog looks on, untouched."

For his first attraction at Universal, "Clive Barker's Freakz," he drew on the theatrical tradition of the carnival freak show, which always created intense audience anticipation through blatant, hyperbolic oversell. Barker, appropriately, played the barker and, via video monitors, warned the waiting throngs of the unspeakably disturbing horrors they were about to behold. The actual maze was fairly run-of-the-mill (in the best sideshow tradition), but successful enough to have Universal bring Barker back for two more Halloween shows: "Clive Barker's Hell" (1999) and "Clive Barker's Harvest" (2000).

The challenges ended up being more logistical than conceptual. "You're mounting a piece of theater with forty people, many of them masked, many of them having to do pretty difficult things – not dramatically difficult, but physically difficult. For a period of five or six hours you need these young kids – because they're the only ones who will take pleasure at being put on a bungee cord and dropped down every three seconds on someone's head," says Barker, who admits that it was "quite an experience to learn what worked and what didn't. It's something you also learn making horror movies – sometimes you can completely outwit yourself by trying to be too sophisticated."

So what works?

" 'Boo!' works." He laughs. "That's it in a nutshell. You can talk all you want about setting up atmosphere, and surprising people with subtle imagery, but what really works is turning the lights out and touching people."

Of course, unless you want to risk charges of legal battery, you can't actually touch anyone, at least not with your hands. And the proscription cuts both ways. During my Halloween visit to the Spookyworld theme park in Foxboro, Massachusetts, I was genuinely surprised at the number of posted signs threatening prosecution if patrons got too up close and personal with the employee-spooks. So what's a shockmeister to do? "You *can* spray people with water," Barker offers, helpfully. "And you can cause people to knock into each other, or into the walls." Universal had no problems with the gruesomer elements of Barker's presentation but insisted on a couple of tactical modifications. "We had a corridor full of holes with various objects that touched people, and some women complained of infringement of their personal space." I bring up the case of a female visitor to the Universal Studios Florida Halloween event, who, a few years earlier, filed suit against the park, claiming she had been unduly traumatized by a make-believe Halloween chain-saw killer.

Barker just shakes his head, incredulous. "God only knows why some people go into a haunted house in the first place."

But his perplexity hints at a possible answer. Haunted houses engage us on a multiplicity of levels, many of them reflecting anxiety and ambivalence about the Good Life, feelings that are playfully exorcised through rituals simulating the Horrible Death. And the most awful death of all, the one we all have to live with, is the death of a sense of community and meaningful social interaction. As American communities become more transient and impersonal, more virtual than visceral, and as civic participation wanes at all levels, the appeal of Halloween rituals may not be so mysterious after all. However empty your neighborhood may appear, at least in a haunted house, there's *always* somebody home.

FOUR

# THE DEVIL ON CASTRO STREET
*And Other Skirmishes in the Culture Wars*

O MATTER THE TIME of the year, it was always a bit like Halloween at the Black Cat Café.

The popular hangout in San Francisco's North Beach had long been a bohemian haunt – a completely unsupernatural haunt, to be sure, even though it had chosen one of the major icons of Halloween as both its name and trademark, and Halloween was always its biggest night of the year. An irrepressible drag entertainer named José Sarria both waited on tables and, weekly, performed his own travesty renditions of operas like *Carmen*; of course, he always presided over Halloween. Sarria was also a pioneering gay activist who injected stinging political commentary into his performances, always enjoined Black Cat audiences to hold hands and sing "God Save Us Nellie Queens" (to the patriotic tune of "My Country 'Tis of Thee"), and encouraged men shaken down on "morals charges" to demand jury trials, in which the lack of evidence would be apparent. He also had the supreme temerity (at least in the view of local authorities) to run for the San Francisco board of supervisors in 1961, garnering a stunning seven thousand votes. Sarria didn't win, but he sent a message – a message that earned him the everlasting enmity of the San Francisco powers-that-were.

In the years after World War II, it was a crime to knowingly, or even unknowingly, sell liquor to a homosexual in California. Even the smallest demonstrations of affection between persons of the same sex could be cause for arrest. Gay bars had to operate with all the precautions and warning systems of speakeasies during Prohibition. As elsewhere in America, bar raids were frequent in San Francisco, but because of the unusually large gay population in the city, there were all that many more people (gay and straight) to be offended by overzealous vice squads. Gay men and women had gravitated to the city in different waves, and for different reasons. The sexual segregation of military life during the war had led untold numbers of enlisted people to discover, or at least come to terms with, their sexual orientation, and San Francisco was the frequent point of reentry to the civilian world for those who had served in the Pacific theater. The magnetic presence of Beat culture in the fifties attracted thousands eager to pursue the unconventional. San Francisco seemed open-minded and more tolerant than other American cities — even if its police had ideas of their own.

There was, however, a special exception to the draconian power of the vice squad. "One night a year, like a chapter from a Cinderella story, the police would bestow a free night upon the homosexuals," observed historian Randy Shilts in *The Mayor of Castro Street*, the biography of assassinated gay city supervisor Harvey Milk. The "free night" was October 31, and the date was only appropriate, wrote Shilts, since "gays did, after all, live most of their lives behind masks."

Halloween is widely celebrated as a gay high holy day, but perhaps nowhere as passionately as in San Francisco, where the historic tensions between the gay community and the authorities gave and continue to give the proceedings a special, feverish intensity. By the early sixties, the city's heavily Irish Catholic police department, in cooperation with the state's Alcohol Beverage Control Commission, had pursued the Black Cat and its habituées with Javert-like zeal for fifteen years. Worn down after prolonged cat-and-mouse conflict and the crippling legal bills that ensued, the Black Cat lost the fight, along with its liquor license, on Halloween 1963. The officials had chosen the day with obvious and sadistic relish.

Two thousand people showed up anyway and celebrated with soft drinks and cider. It was a classic San Francisco Halloween, even without the customary inebriation. According to José Sarria's biographer Michael R. Gorman, "Twelve police officers patrolled in and around the bar. Mink coats and diamonds mixed with T-shirts, leather chaps, and motorcycle boots. There were tourists and students and businessmen, straight couples and gay couples, all gathered to say goodbye to a San Francisco institution."

But for many of the costumed revelers, those who wore the most elegant gowns and glitter, midnight would mark more than just the death of the Black Cat. Like Cinderella's bejeweled carriage, they would all change back into pumpkins – or else. At the stroke of twelve on Halloween, cross-dressing would, once more, become a crime.

In the years before the defiant Stonewall riots of 1969, in which Greenwich Village drag queens violently refused to acquiesce to police harassment, the closet was brutally enforced.

Fortunately, the closet had plenty of costumes.

The outsize attention the media bestows upon transvestites at Halloween parades and gay pride celebrations makes a certain, more assimilationist strata of the gay world cringe, but drag queens have always been in the forefront of gay activism, if only because of their intrinsically heightened visibility. In New York, the now-legendary Greenwich Village Halloween Parade, founded in 1973, took on a gay coloration because of its proximity to the West Village's large homosexual population and the concurrent October 31 revels on Christopher Street, New York's prime gay commercial strip. Originally the brainchild of gifted puppeteer and mask maker Ralph

Lee, who wanted to create a meaningful, mythologically resonant Halloween celebration for his own as well as for neighborhood children, the pageant included dramatically oversized puppets and effigies, and wound through the narrow streets of the Greenwich Village historic district to the initial delight of residents (though later growing pains, traffic disruptions, and rowdyism would sorely tax community support and necessitate a radical change of venue and leadership). An unprecedentedly creative piece of street theater, it won Lee a special Obie Award in 1974. The parade also captured the imagination of the gay population, who became enthusiastic participants in the design, construction, and deployment of the giant puppets, as well as costumed (and often rather uncostumed) participants. As the event's premier chronicler, Jack Kugelmass, has observed, "Unlike most parades, the Village Halloween Parade makes no claim to respectability. Rather than challenge the city by occupying elite turf and marching up Fifth Avenue – the typical route of ethnic parades – the Halloween parade consecrates its own terrain. And unlike other parades, this dramatization of boundaries, in its origins, defined not an ethnic group but a way of life, particularly a Bohemian, artistic, and, frequently, gay way of life."

In San Francisco, where Halloween had traditionally been far more politicized, a distinctly over-the-top drag aesthetic developed, partially in response to archaic laws against posing as a member of the opposite sex. Since travesty drag didn't fool anybody, it couldn't be considered a legitimate attempt at identity fraud (José Sarria famously admonished cross-dressers to always wear a discreet tag stating I AM A BOY, just to stay legal). Like country quilts, vintage carousels, customized cars, and Christmas trees, drag evolved into a true folk art, a singular hybrid of handicraft and chutzpah.

A search through the collections of the Gay, Lesbian, Bisexual and Transgender Historical Society of Northern California for artifacts of San Francisco's Halloween history reveals that the holiday pervades all archival categories. Instead of having a file of its own, Halloween is everywhere: in personal papers and scrapbooks, in photographs, in the donated records and minutes of activist organizations, in advertising and ephemera.

The personal photo albums are especially fascinating, and oddly poignant. One belonged to a lesbian and includes her snapshots of a World War II Halloween party in a women's barracks. The same-sex camaraderie is evident as the women share bottled beer, show off simple costumes, and smile for the camera. A framed portrait of a male military figure has been prankishly overlaid with a ghastly death's-head. One of the women has metamorphosed into "Madame La Zonga," a fortune-teller, and sits on the floor in a corner, solemnly divining fates.

Another album is full of color photos, circa 1960, showing a circle of friends proudly displaying their Halloween finery, apparently just before a night on the town. There are several attractive young men, posing in various degrees of undress as an impressively winged angel, a silver-skinned Bacchus, and another whose costume consists only of a plumed headdress, a floor-length cape, and something that is not exactly a fig leaf, but which might be more accurately termed a figpiece. The drag queens range from southern plantation belles to demure debutantes to an elaborately realized Elizabeth I (with a strong assist from Bette Davis), whose enveloping raiment of velvet and brocade is more akin to a parade float than a costume. Like many of the creations captured in the snapshots, it probably took weeks to build.

In the recollection of one local observer of the sixties and seventies, who identifies himself only as Uncle Donald, "There was no organized event for gays on Halloween, but many of the downtown and Polk Street bars planned appropriate festivities, including costume contests. Drag queens and their 'male' escorts (usually in tuxedos) would rent limousines and drive from bar to bar showing off their elaborate creations. The custom grew in popularity and people would gather outside bars and watch the exotic parade of furs and rhinestones and feathers and glamour." The custom became so popular that the limousines eventually gave way to full-size buses that shuttled between bars. Apart from the public revelries, private drag parties, some staged as nonprofit fund-raisers, also became popular in the days leading up to October 31. In 1965, José Sarria founded the Imperial Court, now an international organization with nearly seventy chapters, "baronies" and "ducals," all dedicated to keeping alive on a year-round basis the gender-bending spirit that had been so cruelly suppressed at the Black Cat Café on Halloween 1962. The Court system's flair for pomp and circumstance has had a perceptible influence on San Francisco's Halloween rituals.

"It's a once in a year chance for men to let their hair down, or put it up," explained Mark Lagasse, one of the organizers of a more recent costume bash celebrating an imaginary San Francisco socialite named Charlotta Manure each October. "It's a very glamorous event, a time to see and be seen," Lagasse told the *San Francisco Sentinel*. "Most of these men go to the gym religiously and are very concerned with how they look to begin with. This party gives them a chance to compete in a completely different way, and a lot of otherwise butch men really get into it. Hundreds of dollars are spent on jewels and sequins every Halloween."[11]

11. Even the most elaborate Halloween costumes tend to be temporary assemblages, but San Francisco is fortunate to have a theatrical institution in which the city's historic flair for outrageous dressing up is lovingly enshrined on a year-round basis. The musical revue *Beach Blanket Babylon*, created in the 1970s by the inspired San Francisco impresario Steve Silver, is still running strong in North Beach – a nonstop pageant of towering headdresses and campy cutting-up, well worth the attention of anyone (gay or straight), with even a passing interest in the carnivalesque. While not a drag show, it manages nonetheless to capture the essence of San Francisco's drag tradition in an ongoing, living celebration.

The new sexual openness of the sixties and seventies had brought another wave of gay migration to San Francisco, far less closeted than before, and the tumultuous politics of the Vietnam era made it clear that almost anything could happen in the streets. All this affected the way Halloween was celebrated in San Francisco. If many people came to the city with flowers in their hair, then a good number also ended up replacing the flowers with tiaras. But beyond the ubiquitous cross-dressers, other sartorial nonconformists – leathermen, cowboys, and uniform fetishists – brought their own theatrical styles to the holiday, often with no more than a somewhat glorified incarnation of their ordinary weekend wear. Nudity, or its near-equivalent, was a costume all its own, celebrated at another traditional Halloween-week San Francisco event, the Exotic Erotic Ball. Distinctions between the sexually ambiguous and the unambiguously sexual frequently blurred at Halloween; as cross-dressing diva Ru Paul has famously observed, "You're born naked, but after that, everything is drag."

Gay liberation made sexual nonconformists more visible than ever, and people who wanted to see them – for whatever reason – knew exactly what time of the year to do it.

In 1976, someone's idea of a San Francisco Halloween prank was to set off tear-gas canisters on Polk Street. Arson directed against gay establishments in San Francisco was all too common. The same year, gay homicides accounted for a full 10 per cent of the city's murder rate. A nationwide antigay backlash was in full swing by 1977, when former Miss America Anita Bryant attempted to resurrect her lagging media career by leading a Florida crusade to repeal gay-rights legislation. The repeal succeeded, but Bryant ended up losing her job as spokesperson for the Florida Citrus Growers Association after a gay-led boycott of Florida orange juice. She also became an inevitable (and irresistible) object for drag travesty at Halloween.

Meanwhile, the center of gay life in San Francisco had gravitated to the former working-class neighborhood of Eureka Valley, now familiarly called the Castro, after its main business street. The owner of Cliff's Variety Store already had a long-established Halloween event, which catered to the neighborhood kids. The store windows were filled with mechanical window displays, and a flatbed trailer became the stage for costume and pie-eating contests. The street was blocked off, and the newer, gay residents started congregating on Castro as well.

Polk Street Halloweens had become crowded and menacing, with gawkers often outnumbering the celebrants. In 1978, Republican state senator John Briggs had sponsored a mean-spirited ballot initiative that would ban gays from teaching in the California school system. Near the end of the rancorous campaign, Briggs attempted to confront Halloween revelers for a photo opportunity, "because this is a children's night and I'm interested in children." Not wanting to incite a riot, city officials, including the mayor and police chief, confronted Briggs personally and convinced him to celebrate Halloween elsewhere for his own safety. "Just fifteen years ago that night," wrote Randy Shilts, "the police and city authorities had forced the Black Cat to close. The confrontation between Briggs and city authorities on Halloween 1978 was but another indication of how fully the tables had turned since that Halloween in 1963."

Among the officials in the preemptive delegation was gay city supervisor Harvey Milk. A few weeks later, a former policeman and supervisor named Dan White would enter City Hall and shoot both the mayor and Milk in cold blood.

Violence against gays always appeared more pronounced at Halloween, but in fact was a year-round plague. The emergence of AIDS in the early 1980s only deepened the gay community's sense of siege. Community United Against Violence (CUAV) was founded in San Francisco in 1979 as a grassroots mobilization to raise awareness and provide practical services. Halloween on Castro Street soon became a major annual project. CUAV began training and coordinating volunteer street monitors to spot weapons, defuse skirmishes, and aid the injured.

Halloween 1982 saw a sudden influx of large groups of youths, as many as one hundred in a pack, yelling antigay epithets and vandalizing storefronts, according to CUAV's Diana Christensen, who wrote a regular column for the *Bay Area Reporter*, one of San Francisco's weekly gay newspapers. In 1983 there were more but smaller gangs, and 1984 set a record for the sheer number of weapons in the crowd, some carried, defensively, by gay people themselves. In a pre-Halloween column that year, Christensen had warned that bashers came camouflaged, in costume. "Attackers dress as baseball players carrying bats, as golfers carrying clubs, and as the elderly with canes."

Few street monitors from 1983 returned, citing combat fatigue. Christensen quoted her own roommate as likening the assignment to "sticking me into Vietnam with nothing more than a sweatshirt with a witch on it!" That night, "Pipes, baseball bats, knives, guns and other assorted lethal weapons were brought into the Castro by the dozens," Christensen wrote, citing a police captain's observation that, "considering the number of weapons confiscated already filled the back of a patrol car, it was a wonder more violent incidents hadn't occurred." Even a machete was confiscated. "But violent incidents did ensue and weapons were used," Christensen reported. "One man scrambled away from the crowd, bleeding profusely from facial cuts caused by the broken bottle that had been smashed into his face." The team's radio log for the half-hour period between nine-fourteen and nine-forty-four P.M. included reports of brass knuckles and chains being spotted and confiscated, and someone spraying Lysol into revelers' faces.

Christensen's published account of the 1984 event is a surreal montage, describing such things as Annette Funicello and "Mod Squad" impersonators (who curtsied demurely to the crowd when they weren't lasciviously lifting their skirts); a bevy of ersatz 1930s bathing beauties, bouncing their beach balls along the street; a real neighborhood waitress who periodically flashed real breasts – all juxtaposed over genuine scenes of random violence, like the young man who suddenly realized he had just been stabbed in the arm, without ever seeing the perpetrator.

Similar chaos erupted the following year in San Francisco, and in New York, Ralph Lee decided to abandon the Greenwich Village parade entirely after police moved it out of the historic far West Village and into the modern commercial sluice of lower Sixth Avenue, with viewers separated from paraders by intimidating barricades. As Lee told the *New York Times*, "In its early years, the parade had a wonderful spontaneity between onlookers and marchers, and there was no separation between the two. But the number of onlookers began to overwhelm the participants, and that's what killed it for me."

In both New York and San Francisco, it was clear that the next October 31 celebration would not be conducted as usual. Direction of the New York parade was assumed by Jeanne Fleming, an experienced event producer with a large estate in Duchess County far better suited for the construction of large-scale, television-friendly floats and props than Lee's studio at the Westbeth artists' housing project in the Village. On October 18, 1986, CUAV issued an open letter on the subject of Halloween.

For five years, CUAV staff and volunteers have been in the streets Halloween night, taking on an increasingly dangerous physical risk in order to help protect members of our community. What we have seen, however, is not a decrease in Halloween hostilities but an intensification of the danger. Last year, CUAV monitors helped confiscate over 100 weapons, including knives, bats, live guns and machetes. We have been the eyes and ears of the Police, assuming the very real risk of serious bodily injury or worse.

This year, the Board and staff of CUAV have decided we can no longer risk the escalating danger of a highly visible street presence on Halloween and we are therefore changing our role.

For the first time, a liaison agreement with the San Francisco Police Department would pair volunteer monitors with patrolmen. The "onus of confronting assailants and confiscating weapons will be on the Police this year – not us," the letter explained. The number of volunteers was reduced, and it was agreed that no volunteer would work independently of a police officer partner. Additionally, photographer teams were posted in both the Polk and Castro neighborhoods. The street-level photographers would operate co-vertly, identifying bashers or potential attackers. Highly visible telephoto teams in second-story windows and on rooftops were meant to be frankly intimidating. Volunteer observer-assistance teams, including attorneys, were enlisted to simply document events. Medical units were expanded, and walkie-talkies were linked to an emergency CB radio network. Finally, CUAV chair Carl MacMillin just urged people to stay away. "We encourage people to attend private gatherings or the many organized events in the city on Halloween," he said in a press release. "Although the overwhelming majority of people, straight and gay, come out on Halloween to enjoy the celebration as good neighbors, the crowded conditions and the actions of a violent few can make these areas dangerous and very unpleasant."

By 1990, the annual crowds trying to squeeze into a few short blocks on Castro Street had grown bigger than ever, an estimated quarter-million people jamming the upper Market Street area. The usual headaches were ameliorated somewhat by the presence of the Sisters of Perpetual Indulgence, a group of clownish transvestites in nun's habits whose outrageous street theater and media savvy had proved an effective tool for fund-raising and community works. (The Sisters are also, without doubt, the only nonprofit charity to ever be included on an official list of papal heretics, due to their eyebrow-raising antics during the pope's visit to San Francisco in 1987.) In cooperation with CUAV, the Sisters erected an outdoor stage, and, for the first time, provided some focused entertainment, while proclaiming the need for gays and lesbians to "take back" Halloween. According to Sisters member Ken Bunch, "more than eighty per cent of the people who come out are straight people who come to gawk at the queers." This year, fifteen blocks were cordoned off by police, instead of the usual four. At each barricade entrance, donations were solicited for AIDS agencies and activist organizations.

But Castro Street wasn't the only large-scale Halloween event that evening. The yearly spectacle had also drawn the excited interest of Texas televangelist Larry Lea, a protégé of Oral Roberts, and his San Jose associate Richard Bernal. The ministers both saw the chance for a high-profile evangelical counterevent. As Bernal told the *Wall Street Journal*, San Francisco was a city "where it's easier to get a condom than it is to get a Bible," and that a full-scale exorcism was in order. "We're not talking about street-level demons here. These are high-ranking evil spirits."

Conjuring the image of the devil himself prowling Castro Street worked like a New Age charm in capturing media attention, and Lea's plans to bring ten thousand "Prayer Warriors" to the Civic Center Auditorium made headlines across the country. The *San Francisco Chronicle* described the trademark style of Lea's "Prayer

Breakthrough" gatherings: "Amid fervent praying, military rhetoric, and 'speaking in tongues,' believers attempt to conquer Satanic princes and specific 'territorial spirits' holding sway over various metropolitan areas."

In 1990, the gay community had already suffered eight years of AIDS devastation and regular scapegoating by conservative Christians. Larry Lea and his followers were simply not welcome in San Francisco, and especially not on Halloween. An ad hoc group called GHOST – Grand Homosexual Outrage at Sickening Televangelists – was formed by members of the activist organization Queer Nation, who recruited gays, Wiccans, and pro-choice groups to demonstrate. Sixty-five hundred Prayer Warriors actually showed up. "Police in riot helmets stood behind steel barricades that separated the arriving worshipers from several hundred protestors determined to vent their anger," reported the *San Francisco Examiner*. "Lea's followers were showered first with chants and slogans, and later with eggs and fruit. The hostile protestors began with creative chants such as 'The people, perverted, will never be converted,' and 'Bring back the lions,' but those soon deteriorated into shouted obscenities."

The media salivated, but those working on the street-level front lines of Halloween were convinced that some basic changes were in order. The following summer, CUAV program coordinator Jill Tregor informed her board of directors that "most gay men and lesbians found the whole thing so frightening and unpleasant that they stayed away from their own neighborhood and therefore did not take part in a celebration that was started within the community." The basic problem, wrote Tregor, was that Halloween on Castro Street was an event that "occurs to some extent spontaneously, meaning that no one sponsors the event or takes any responsibility for it." Amazingly, no street permits had ever been authorized for Halloween; instead, "the streets were closed on a so-called 'emergency' basis." Volunteers "probably prevented even more violence from occurring, but did nothing to actually bring focus or real control to the event."

The Sisters of Perpetual Indulgence felt a certain testy sense of ownership, given their positive innovations of the previous year, and a reported fifteen thousand dollars in one-dollar donations. CUAV gingerly negotiated with the city, the Sisters, and another group that had taken the initiative to actually obtain a city permit for Halloween 1991. The city accepted insurance liability, and CUAV produced the event. Violence dropped dramatically, and fundraising soared to thirty-five thousand dollars. Meanwhile, evangelist Larry Lea returned to the city he called "a graveyard of preachers and churches" for another prayer storm, this time held at Candlestick Park baseball stadium – about as far from Castro Street as one can get and still be in San Francisco. A highlight of the show was the appearance of one of the previous year's pagan protesters, who had converted to Christianity after "intense discussions" with Richard Bernal.

Protests against the perceived Halloween interloper cooled considerably that year, but elsewhere around the country, evangelicals began finding innovative ways to make hay from the holiday.

In Dennis, Massachusetts, many visitors to the "Haunted House on Hell Street" were upset when the usual monsters, strobe lights, and fog machines quickly gave way to a series of grisly moral lessons. A coffin creaked open to reveal a blood-soaked young man who must witness his own funeral, his death the result of drunk driving. A bloody murder victim pulled the switch on his killer's electric chair. And finally, the visitors were ushered into hell itself, where, as the *Boston Globe* described the scene, "a young woman writhes on a hospital gurney yelling, 'Where is my baby?' An attending physician hands her what appears to be a small, blood-covered object – presumably an aborted fetus – and says, 'Here, you knew what you were doing when you had the abortion.' Then a teen-age girl steps forward and says, 'I would have been that child.'"

The haunted house was sponsored by the Victory Chapel Christian Fellowship Church, and immediately raised the ire of the abortion-rights organizations Mass Choice and the Cape Cod Women's Agenda. A Mass Choice representative told the press, "Our objection principally is that this is being billed as family entertainment and it clearly is not. There is no way to know what you will see when you enter is graphic and grisly and is proselytizing for a particular point of view. In particular, it equates criminal acts – like drunk driving and murder – with abortion, which is not illegal." The sponsoring church offered no apologies.

Just as garden-variety haunted houses were widely imitated by fund-raising organizations in the 1970s, fundamentalist "hell houses" caught on as Halloween events (or anti-Halloween events) for the 1990s. One of the most controversial was a 1995 version in Arvada, Colorado, sponsored by the Abundant Life Christian Center. In addition to the obligatory abortion and drunk-driving skits, this one also included a satanic human sacrifice and the funeral of an AIDS patient presented as a warning against homosexuality. Animal entrails in a bloody dish were employed to simulate a mangled fetus. The Colorado Council of Churches registered a formal protest, noting that "We have several denominations that oppose abortion and homosexuality, but none of them use these kind of tactics. This reeks of aggression, violence and hatred that could traumatize youth rather than teaching them understanding and love." A more spontaneous protest was mounted by graffiti artists, who spray-painted slogans like JESUS DIED FOR HIS SINS – NOT MINE on the church. Julian Rush, director of the Colorado AIDS Project and a United Methodist minister, accused the church of "catering to the lowest levels of voyeurism, and blaming victims for the sorrows and tragedies of the world." Publicity for Hell House was overwhelming, and Abundant Life marketed a 280-page manual with a production kit (cost: $149) for other churches eager to get into the brimstone business.

In Lilburn, Georgia, the same Halloween, the First Baptist Church's Judgment House allowed that a teenage girl with AIDS could indeed go to heaven, as long as she contracted the disease from a blood transfusion and not from sex. But her boyfriend, who killed himself from grief, went directly to hell. Electric heaters were used to make damnation feel all the more real. The attraction drew forty-three hundred visitors. One mother told the *Atlanta Constitution* of her fourteen-year-old daughter's distress upon returning from Judgment House. "I think the depiction of hell was her deepest concern. She was worried. She was confused." In the family's own, Presbyterian tradition, she said, "God is loving, trusting, compassionate, forgiving, and she saw this side [of Christianity] where she thought if you didn't do absolutely everything right you would burn in hell."

In Stockbridge, Georgia, beginning with Halloween 1992, a far more elaborate vision of hell, "Tribulation Trail," was presented outdoors on a mile-and-a-half-long woodland path. By 1997, according to the *Atlanta Journal and Constitution*, the event employed over three hundred members of the Metro Heights Baptist Church as actors, set builders, concession vendors, and traffic controllers. Attendance was estimated at twenty thousand. "No cute baby-faced devils with quilted red costumes for these amateur actors," religion writer Gayle White reported. "These are dark demons from the depths of hell, dragging away those who flunk the test at the magnificent Great White Throne of Judgment." The extravaganza also included dramatic depictions of the Antichrist and the Rapture, and a counseling tent at the end of the trail provided information for people interested in conversion.

Not every church-sponsored Halloween haunt involves evangelizing, and many are very similar to the walk-through mazes sponsored by other nonprofit agencies. However, a certain level of cognitive, cultural, and spiritual dissonance can result when ghouls and goblins invade sacred space. "A madman in the pulpit at the first United Methodist Church in Oak Park?" asked *Chicago Tribune* religion writer Michael Hirsley, observing the trend in 1993. "Worms and 'bloody finger' sandwiches in the school gym at St. Matthew Lutheran Church in Lake Zurich? Severed heads and a giant gorilla in the basement of St. Benedict Roman Catholic Church in Chicago?" But all these and more were indeed available at mainstream religious institutions all around metropolitan Chicago, all of which shrugged off the occasional conservative complaint. As the Reverend David Owens, pastor of the First Congregational Church in Wilmette, Illinois, noted, "The bottom line is that we recognize the terror and wonder of the spiritual world. What better place to celebrate that than in the church?" Halloween, he maintained, offered "a chance to deal symbolically and imaginatively with the terror and violence all around us."

Real-world violence certainly fueled the grassroots imagination of Halloween celebrants all across the country in 1994, when the most coveted and publicized costumes were, to the dismay of most commentators, a blood-soaked O. J. Simpson and his savagely murdered ex-wife, Nicole. When Morris Costumes, the North Carolina-based mega-manufacturer of masks and Halloween gear, determined that it would be impossible to license Simpson's image, bootleggers enthusiastically filled the vacuum. Licensed or not, weird rubber masks in O.J.'s image sold out rapidly wherever they could be found, especially in Southern California, the red-hot epicenter of the Simpson circus. The manager of a costume shop in Laguna Niguel told the *Los Angeles Times* that "I've had calls about blonde 'Nicole' wigs, dark makeup, Afro wigs, big butcher knives, and, of course, the O.J. mask." Another costume vendor, in

Fullerton, California, marketed football jerseys "similar to the kind Simpson wore with the USC Trojans and the Buffalo Bills – only these are splattered with fake blood and for legal reasons bear a different number," the *Times* reported.

Generic latex gash wounds, a longtime staple of costume and joke shops, were in sudden demand, and "some have even bought neck prostheses that have wounds carved into them," noted the *Chicago Tribune*.

Nicole Simpson's sister, Denise Brown, issued an immediate appeal to the public to boycott products that exploited the crime, but the media had already turned the case into the season's most sensational piece of infotainment. The demand for O.J. Halloween costumes was so intense that "Some consumers who haven't come across any bootlegged masks have settled for [any] that depict black men," including Mike Tyson and, in a pinch, even the swarthy Libyan leader Muammar Gadhafi.

"We just want to win a few couples' costume contests and have a few laughs," one twenty-year-old man told the *Chicago Tribune*. His twenty-two-year-old girlfriend hadn't quite decided if she wanted to dress as Nicole for Halloween, but was leaning in that direction. "It's not making fun of Nicole's death," she said. However, "You're supposed to bring all the horror out at Halloween." But one cannot help but question the precise humor/horror ratio of one costume concept reported by the press: a bloody effigy of the throat-slashed Nicole, gaily reconstructed as a bloody Pez candy dispenser.

"This isn't even the sickest costume we've sold," said a Fullerton, California, dealer. "We had a couple who dressed as JFK and Jackie Kennedy and wanted to put blood and brain matter on their suits so they could recreate Dallas." The *San Francisco Chronicle* noted the 1994 revisitation of the Richard Nixon disguise, so popular in the Watergate area. Those so disposed could now go for "an updated version, in honor of the late president's passing this year: the dead

Nixon mask, a grayish mass of coffin-aged skin and decayed nose." Another popular 1994 costume was Lorena Bobbitt, the infamous penis-chopper, macabrely glamorized with gleaming cutlery and a blood-dripping sandwich bag in lieu of a designer purse.

Since Halloween has always provided an open season on propriety and authority, tasteless Halloween costumes may simply be an extension of the pranking tradition. Reports of property vandalism are fairly rare these days, but Halloween assaults on taste and sensibility are extremely common. Author/filmmaker Clive Barker, who maintains he has never worn a Halloween costume, despite his long association with dark fantasy ("The ideal Clive Barker costume would be the Invisible Man, without his clothes on," he says), shares his still-vivid recollection of a West Hollywood Halloween celebration that coincided with the trial of Erik and Lyle Menendez for the murders of their parents. "Gay men were watching the trial on Court TV because the sons were cute, and all that," Barker says. On Santa Monica Boulevard, he saw "two drag queens playing the corpses of the Menendez mother and father, complete with tombstones on their heads. They were rotting, gray, and full of bullet holes. The punchline was, they were doing this carrying bowls of berries and cream, because, you remember, the parents were killed while they were eating berries and cream. It was hysterically funny – and a complete release from the horrible, grisly, terrible reality." Similarly ghoulish costumes with tombstone headdresses were reported following the anorexia death of pop singer Karen Carpenter in 1983.

Barker attributes the trademark gay penchant for black humor, in part, to the subculture's recent confrontation with death and desolation in the age of AIDS. "If we can somehow play with death, that empowers us, and gives us a way to say we're not going to give in. Gay men and women have been incredibly smart over the years in using humor to take the sting out of death." He admits, however, that a travesty spectacle like the José and Kitty Menendez costumes tends to be more spontaneous than cerebrated. "I don't think anyone's really intellectualizing when they're dressing up and smoking a joint and putting on a mask," Barker says.

Nonetheless, Halloween costumes and customs still manage to speak volumes about the meaning and purpose of Halloween. Barker recounts how a West Hollywood street celebration provided a personal epiphany and suggests quoting from something he has already written. He retrieves the original typescript of his introduction to the omnibus edition of *The Books of Blood*, describing how he, uncostumed, escorted his companion David Armstrong, who had spent six hours transforming himself into an impressive, erotic gargoyle, "an amalgam of sexual excess and demonic elegance." While "watching the way people's eyes fell on my monstrous companion – the mingling of delight and revulsion – I began to remember what made me a horror writer . . . knowing the words I was putting on the page would stop people in their tracks, as my lover's curious beauty was now doing; make them wonder, perhaps, if the line between what they feared and what they took pleasure in was not a good deal finer than they'd once imagined."

There is one line that has become exceedingly fine in recent years, and subject to endless and excruciating analysis: the political correctness of Halloween costumes.

In 1993, the Iowa City school system raised a number of eyebrows when it sent parents a letter admonishing them to discourage their children from wearing costumes that might offend members of a wide variety of cultural and ethnic groups. Categories officially frowned upon included "Gypsy, American Indian princess, African, witch, old man, differently abled person, East Indian, slave, hobo, devil, old woman." The following year, after citing several local examples of inappropriate disguises, the *Chicago Tribune* concluded that the only really safe costume might well be a stalk of broccoli.

Despite the nonobservance of Halloween by mainstream religions, issues of church/state separation have also fueled controversies about the place of Halloween in public schools. A particularly
angry confrontation erupted in 1995, when the Los Altos, California, school system announced that it was banning traditional
October 31 activities in the classroom to avoid the appearance of
endorsing a religious holiday. The issue had been simmering for two
years after complaints about the inclusion of Christmas carols in a
winter concert. Now, a different group of parents objected to their
children being exposed to supernatural imagery and paganism.
"Teaching about Halloween will fall under guidelines about teaching about religious beliefs and customs," said school board president
Phil Faillace. "And school time may not be used to celebrate
Halloween, just as it may not be used to celebrate Easter, Yom
Kippur, or Ramadan."

Many parents were shocked by what they perceived as the heavy-
handed quashing of a secular holiday. "My kids are really upset,"
said one father. "I can understand concern about a religious aspect,
but they just wanted to dress up as cartoon characters." A crowd of
eight hundred parents and children, many in costumes, jammed a
school trustees meeting to make their pro-Halloween stance perfectly clear. The complaining parents were not much in evidence,
although an evangelical minister from San Jose, a former pagan who
called himself "the witch who switched," testified that his previous
fascination with satanism developed "from playing Halloween
games, and one thing led to another." The trustees sided with
the majority of parents and reversed their ruling, agreeing that
"Halloween is not a religious holiday, and that ballerinas, witches
and Power Rangers will be welcomed back into the schools on
October 31," according to the *San Francisco Chronicle*.

Similar contretemps have continued to flare up around the
country, and the newsletter *Consumer Trends Reports* recently issued

a caution to businessmen in planning their holiday offerings and inventory:

> Each year as Halloween draws near, more and more special interest groups begin protesting the dark side of Halloween. Goths have been blamed for school shootings; Halloween has pagan beginnings and is counter to many religious teachings. Many parents will not allow their children to dress up as cops and robbers and wield plastic guns. To young consumers, it seems that every year, Boomers come up with more and more rules. Thus, every year the number of politically correct costumes decreases. Remember when you could dress up like an Indian, a witch, a cowboy, a ghost or a hobo without some group or association saying you were demeaning them?

Ethnic groups allegedly maligned by costumes, however, frequently have no problems with traditional Halloween apparel. A Native American store owner in Romeoville, Illinois, told reporters that she proudly rented authentic handmade Ojibwa tribe costumes. "This is part of my heritage, and if people want to dress up in my native costumes, I'm honored."

Of course, the political correctness debate generated a lot of humor, and scores of Web sites cropped up with examples of "objectionable" Halloween costumes. Dracula, for instance, was potentially offensive to Romanians, and also encouraged unprotected exposure to body fluids. The Bride of Frankenstein was being exploited for her husband's infamy, not her own accomplishments. Skeleton costumes might be insensitive to anorexics and famine victims. As for sheeted ghosts . . . well, weren't they just the perfect definition of dead white guys?

Not all "marginalized" groups would necessarily agree with PC precepts. Disabled persons, for instance, now have Internet resources to share ideas for lighthearted, self-spoofing costume ideas that imaginatively incorporate wheelchairs, canes, and crutches. A wheelchair, for instance, might become a throne or a robot or even a spaceship. One contributor to a back-and-neck-injury Web site suggested that a ventriloquist with dummy getup was "perfect for a wheelchair since the ventriloquist sits anyway to make the doll talk." Canes and crutches provide creative opportunities for third legs and other bizarre appendages, and so on. (An amputee acquaintance of this writer once replaced his prosthetic with a pirate's peg leg, to the delight of his friends – and despite the culture cops' inevitable objections.)

However excessive some of the hand-wringing over the propriety of certain disguises became, a few incidents did manage to offend people across political divides. Several universities suspended students and sanctioned fraternities after Halloween 2001 for sporting blackface disguises. The most extreme case occurred at Auburn University in Alabama, where fifteen students received indefinite suspensions, some for face blackening and some for wearing Ku Klux Klan robes at a fraternity party. The students, all white males, posed for photos simulating a lynching that were later posted on the Internet and brought to the attention of the Southern Poverty Law Center, which promptly reposted the images and created the predictable media uproar.

Simultaneously, a very different kind of uproar was generated when seventeen-year-old Christian Silbereis of Ann Arbor, Michigan, showed up at school dressed to the nines . . . as a giant vagina. His mother, a midwife, had fabricated the costume for herself the previous year, and handed it down to her son. The outfit included a pink cape and fetus-imprinted T-shirt as fashion accessories to an upholstered satin vulva stretching down the costume's front. The assistant dean confronted Silbereis and made him remove the outfit, but he later put it back on, just in time to win first prize at the students' costume contest. The school then suspended him for the remainder of the week.

All along, some commentators maintained that the emphasis on offensive costumes, devil worship, and candy tampering was ultimately a red herring. In 1996, Kristine Holmgren, a Presbyterian pastor and commentator for National Public Radio, criticized the tendency of touchy parents to sanitize Halloween while turning a blind eye toward true social problems. "Real evil can be found in the numbers of children living in poverty, the children who are victims of unwanted sexual advances, children born to teenage mothers, children abused, neglected, dropping out of school, dying of violence," she wrote. "So, we examine our children's candy before we let them eat it. It feels like a good thing to do, and it is certainly easier than taking personal responsibility for the real troubles in our community."

In 1989, the *New York Times* took note of the growing trend among alienated young people to turn the trappings of Halloween into a full-time lifestyle. The gothic, or goth, sensibility was flourishing as a cultural accessory to the heavy metal music scene, and performers like Alice Cooper, Kiss, and Marilyn Manson presented themselves in costumes and attitudes previously reserved for October 31. Pale makeup and dark clothes pervaded the subculture. Although conservative critics of the goth scene expressed (and continue to express) alarm at the faux satanism and occult posturing, one child psychiatrist, Dr. Paul King, likened the goth style among teenagers to a defensive "character armor of evil." Another expert, Arnold Markowitz, took the issue of cults seriously, but cautioned that appearances weren't always what they seemed. "Teenagers are often rebellious," he told the *Times*. "A way to do that is by becoming interested in things that are repugnant to society and adults."

One undeniably real social problem at Halloween is alcohol

abuse, which some child experts link generally to an increased prediliction for the occult and macabre. Unlike other drinking holidays like St. Patrick's Day and New Year's Eve, Halloween is a time when younger children are especially likely to be crossing intersections and otherwise dodging traffic. Beginning in 1994, the Berkeley, California-based Trauma Foundation joined with other children's-health-advocacy groups to lobby the Beer Institute, a national trade organization; they launched a cross-country campaign called "Hands Off Halloween" and distributed a sample letter to be sent to local beer vendors.

Dear [Merchant]:

I am writing to ask you to join [name of sponsoring organization] and [x] other local organizations in making Halloween safer for our community's children. We are participating in the national Hands Off Halloween effort and are conducting a Responsible Merchants Campaign in [city].

In recent years, the beer industry has used its considerable promotional resources to turn Halloween into a major drinking holiday. It has created elaborate store displays that use children's favorite Halloween symbols, such as jack-o-lanterns, black cats, bats and ghosts, to market beer. The problem is that children are inevitably drawn to these ads, especially when the promotions include balloons, paper masks, and stickers.

Your beer distributor may have provided you with some of these promotional items. We ask you not to display them. Adults who want to purchase beer for their own parties will do so without the use of gimmicks that appeal to kids.

The gimmicks included some especially elaborate beer promotions by Miller tied in to the Universal Studios monster characters. In one series of ads, Miller bottles were costumed in Dracula's cape, the Mummy's bandages, the Frankenstein's-monster suit (with bolts protruding from the bottle neck). Another, headlined WELCOME TO OUR LITE-MARE, featured a male and female vampire eschewing blood in favor of brew. But the Beer Institute held fast to its position: "Adults have celebrated Halloween long before beer companies began special promotions for the holiday," said Institute president Raymond McGrath in a prepared statement. "There is no evidence – whatsoever – that alcohol misuse increases on Halloween." Nonetheless, Hands Off Halloween had some limited success in convincing 7-Eleven convenience stores and the Anheuser-Busch organization to curb Halloween-themed campaigns.

Many cultural skirmishes in recent decades have involved animal rights, and Halloween is no exception. In 1990, the Louisiana Society for the Prevention of Cruelty to Animals warned pet owners to keep black cats indoors until the end of October, citing a suspicious increase in mysterious cat disappearances around Halloween, as well as a particularly ugly incident several years earlier in which a dead cat was hung by the neck as a party decoration at a well-to-do New Orleans home. The society also placed a moratorium on the adoption of black cats for the same period, speculating that the missing animals might have been sacrificed in voodoo rituals. A dozen years later, similar curbs on cat adoption are still firmly in place at animal shelters across the country (notices announcing seasonal blackouts on black felines appeared at more than one pet store in the Los Angeles area during October 2001). However, animal advocates can take heart in the concurrent, nonviolent inclusion of pets at Halloween. The May 2001 issue of *Consumer Trends Report* alerts vendors to the fact that "many couples are waiting longer to have children, and thus, have the financial means to spend money on their pets . . . consumers are opening their wallets and plopping down large amounts of cash to dress them up for Halloween. Many pet owners will also buy their pooch a new toy or two. Stock up on dog toys shaped like leaves, pumpkins, ghosts and tombstones."

Unfortunately, Halloween bashers are able to cite a long legacy of tragic accidents and mishaps that bolster the view that Halloween is an intrinsically dangerous holiday. In 1981, a twenty-three-year-old Parma, Ohio, man, Ernest Pecek, planned to attend a Halloween party dressed as a vampire. In lieu of a stake in his heart, he attempted to drive a sharp, doubled-edged knife into a pine board concealed under his shirt. The board gave way readily to the blade, as did Pecek's chest wall. Death ensued.

In 1988, Milton Tyree, a forty-one-year-old resident of Cambridge, Massachusetts, donned a Hunchback of Notre Dame costume and shuffled into a neighborhood lounge, a noose knotted around his neck. About twenty amused customers laughed as he climbed on a chair and appeared to attach the end of the noose to an overhead beam before he stepped off the chair. After a few minutes of increasingly nervous laughter, it became apparent that something had gone terribly wrong. It wasn't the rope, which had only been thrown over the beam. Rather, a concealed safety harness beneath Tyree's costume slipped and strangled him. He died in a hospital the following morning.

In 1993, the city of Pasadena, California, was staggered when trick-or-treaters Stephen Coats and Reggie Crawford, both fourteen, and Edgar Evans, thirteen, were mowed down by semiautomatic gunfire on the sidewalk of a residential neighborhood. The two killers had been lying in wait in the bushes, and fled in a nearby car. They were gang members exacting revenge for an earlier shooting, to which the dead boys had no connection whatsoever. The same night, a forty-seven-year-old woman was standing at the altar of a church in central Los Angeles when two teenagers drove past the open doors, yelled "Trick or treat!" and opened fire, grievously wounding the mother of six, who required five hours of abdominal surgery. The following year, Northern Ireland terrorists also called out "Trick or treat!" when they stormed a bar outside of Belfast, brandishing guns. When a woman expressed the opinion that the trick wasn't funny, they killed her, along with six other people.

In 1999, a Buena Park, California, grandfather named Pete Solomona became enraged when a pair of teenagers snatched a plastic pumpkin from his porch. He responded by emerging from the house with a .357 Magnum and shooting to death seventeen-year-old Brandon Ketsdever. A few days before Halloween 2000, television actor Anthony Dwain Lee, thirty-nine, was attending a costume party in the exclusive Benedict Canyon district of Los Angeles. He was wearing a red cape and carried a fake rubber gun, a realistic approximation of a .357 Magnum. Los Angeles Police Department officer Tarriel Hopper was responding to a neighborhood noise complaint when he and Lee came fatally face-to-face through one of the party house windows. Lee allegedly pulled the fake gun from his waistband and pointed it at the officer. Hopper opened fire. Lee was killed by one gunshot to the head and three to his back. Hopper claimed that he acted in self-defense, within department guidelines, and the Los Angeles Commission, in a split vote, eventually agreed. In the meantime, Lee's family hired superstar attorney Johnnie Cochran, of O.J. fame, who filed a one-hundred-million-dollar wrongful-death suit against the city, claiming racial profiling. The case is still pending at the time of this writing.

Beyond individual incidents and tragedies, those looking for evidence of Halloween's essential unruliness need look no further than Detroit, Michigan, which has struggled for decades to control the epidemic of arson traditionally afflicting the city on October 30, or Devil's Night, as it came to be popularly known. A perversely destructive variation on ancient Halloween bonfire rituals, Devil's Night arson reached a peak in 1984 when the fire department responded to at least 350 blazes. The previous year, the *Detroit Free Press* observed that "quite a few of the fires flared up in abandoned houses, a commentary, perhaps, on the number of such eyesores blighting Detroit. Some sociologists might theorize that people wanted to burn away some of the ugliness and speed up the process of change. Other more cynical observers might point to the desire of hard-pressed city homeowners to collect fire insurance." But, the paper sadly concluded, "contemplating the roots of such outbursts – the feelings of hopelessness and despair, boredom with things as they are, defiance of those charged with making it better – provides little comfort as fire sirens scream in the night." Following the 1984 fires, the paper pointedly avoided sociological analysis and urged a law-and-order approach to Halloween Eve arson and crime, including gun control, aggressive prosecution, and more jail cells. An editorial defined the problem as a "human rights" issue: "People are entitled to live in their homes in Detroit without the possibility that some idiot will decide to burn down a vacant building under the cover of Devil's Night and provide the spark that sets occupied homes on fire."

Detroit's decaying city core was already an embarrassment to city officials, and the annual Halloween chaos only exacerbated the city's image problems. Television crews descended on Detroit from places as far afield as Japan to catch the flames on videotape, and hundreds of voyeuristic "fire buffs" had also chosen Detroit as their Hallow-een mecca of choice. As a result, the city was much slower to release fire statistics than it had been. "It seems it's become a national sport to trash the City of Detroit," said Harold Shapiro, chairman of the Board of Police Commissioners, noting the "great delight" the media took in serving up the annual civic barbecue.

Detroit fought back over the next decade, instituting six P.M. curfews for persons under the age of seventeen, as well as volunteer neighborhood patrols. Thousands of abandoned houses were razed, and pre-Halloween police roundups of identified troublemakers cleared the streets of potential offenders. Fires subsided to normal statistical levels, but in 1994 the city had a sudden resurgence of Halloween arson, with 360 fires reported between October 29 and 31. In a renewed community effort, now called Angel's Night, participation in the 1995 volunteer patrols would rise to over thirty thousand, on foot and in vehicles. Another three thousand empty buildings, mostly abandoned autoworkers' housing from the 1930s and 1940s, were torn down between 1996 and 1999. Detroit has, once more, reduced its October arson problem to a relatively normal level, but only with the extraordinary and ongoing efforts of tens of thousands of vigilant citizens, and the permanent equivalent of Halloween martial law for young people. Even as Detroit's mediagenic mayhem was beamed around the globe, Halloween itself began to put down roots in foreign countries with a strong exposure to American popular culture. During the 1980s and 1990s, American-style Halloween imagery regularly cropped up in Japanese advertising, and drunken, boorish businessmen in masks were regular sights on Japanese commuter trains. The Japanese attach no occult significance to the commercial holiday, however; their own Samhain-like ritual occurs in August with the celebration of O-Bon, when ancestral spirits are invited to visit the living, lured by small fires burned on doorsteps.

In France, the legend of the Ankou, a scythe-wielding amalgam of the Grim Reaper and Father Time, has long been part of Brittany's New Year folklore; it evolved, like Halloween, from Celtic antiquity. However, no French equivalent of the October holiday ever took root, and when transplanted Americans tried to introduce trick-or-treating to suburban Paris in the mid 1990s, it was not without some cultural incomprehension. The French tend to prize their privacy, and diminutive monsters entreating invasively at the door are simply not part of any Gallic tradition. "Desperate to end an awkward encounter, a flustered Frenchman said he once tossed a small tin of foie gras into the bag of an equally bewildered American child," the Associated Press reported. But Halloween as a party excuse for French adults quickly spread throughout Latin Quarter bars, propelling the holiday to the second most money-spinning celebration after New Year's Eve. One Parisian shop owner told the *Los Angeles Times* that Halloween "has quickly become popular because it allows the French — who like to think of themselves as rational, faultlessly polite beings — to indulge some of their darker and more macabre fantasies." In 1997, Veuve Clicquot, the legendary champagne prized by Hemingway in his Parisian days, issued a special Halloween bottle (one that never, apparently, came to the attention of Hands Off Halloween).

The cultural collisions, controversies, and occasional catastrophes attending Halloween may simply be hardwired into a holiday forged from the tug of war between glitter and grave dust, the sacred and the profane, order and lawlessness, the mainstream and the marginalized. Conflict and consternation are likely unavoidable in a celebration based on pranks, reversals, and the ritual suspension of propriety. Despite the best (and sometimes worst) efforts of people on all sides of the sociopolitical spectrum, Halloween is a holiday that refuses to play by anyone's rules. Unpredictable and unrepentant, Halloween also remains stubbornly unofficial and underground, and this may be the key to understanding the tumult that regularly erupts in its name. Despite the considerable cultural space Halloween now occupies, despite the billions of dollars it annually spins, and despite the passionate commitment millions devote to the holiday, no legislative body has ever seriously considered making it legal.

FIVE

# HALLOWEEN ON SCREEN

EW HOLIDAYS HAVE A cinematic potential that equals Halloween's. Visually, the subject is unparalleled, if only considered in terms of costume design and art direction. Dramatically, Halloween's ancient roots evoke dark and melodramatic themes, ripe for transformation into film's language of shadow and light. Cinema itself had roots in magic-lantern presentations of the nineteenth century, which frequently evoked the possibility of contact with the spirit world. Apparitions were projected on clouds of smoke to create the illusion that the veil between life and death had been penetrated.

The trick of full animation provided a technological treat for audiences that has now lasted more than a century. Many of the silent cinema's earliest and most indelible images involve the fantastic and the macabre; *The Cabinet of Dr. Caligari*, *Nosferatu*, and *The Phantom of the Opera* are still revived regularly at Halloween.

But, curiously, movies were more than eighty years old before Halloween itself was fully exploited by Hollywood.

In early 1978, producer Irwin Yablans was astonished to learn that the title *Halloween* had never been used for a feature film. The low-budget picture that he and his partner, Moustapha Akkad, were then producing had the working title of *The Babysitter Murders*, and was set on Halloween. Only the 1966 half-hour television special

*It's the Great Pumpkin, Charlie Brown* had previously attempted a complete story line revolving around the holiday.

Although Halloween was not unknown to earlier screenwriters and directors, it had always been used as atmosphere, never as a central subject. The holiday made its first, fleeting screen appearance in the 1914 film *The Three of Us*, produced by by B. A. Rolfe Photoplays, Inc., based on a 1906 play by Rachel Crothers, and starring Mabel Talliafaro. The film included a Halloween dance set in a Colorado mining town. Four years later, the Famous Players-Lasky Corporation produced *The Way of a Man with a Maid*. Directed by Donald Crisp and based on a *Saturday Evening Post* story by Ida M. Evans, the film spotlighted a lavish Halloween party. In the 1920 Ebony Film Corporation production *Do the Dead Talk?*, actress Herminia France startled audiences by setting her clothes on fire while preparing a jack-o'-lantern.

Halloween also figured as a background element in 1922's *At the Sign of the Jack O'Lantern*, a Remco Film Company mystery-comedy involving a will, an inheritance, and a haunted house. Tiffany Productions' *Cheaters* (1927), a crime melodrama directed by Oscar Apfel, featured a Halloween celebration. In 1931, *Halloween* was used for the first time as a film title, in this case for an animated short produced by Charles Mintz and Amadee J. Van Beuren and starring their popular character Toby the Pup.

The next Halloween film on record was also a cartoon, *Betty Boop's Halloween Party* (1933). Directed by Dave Fleischer, it spotlighted the irrepressible Ms. Boop's October 31 festivities, thrown for a group of animal friends and a neighborhood scarecrow but interrupted by the appearance of a voracious gorilla, who scarfs down a full tub of bobbing apples and must be repelled. *Betty Boop's Halloween Party* features some vintage Fleischer imagery: scudding clouds that throw shadows of classic Halloween icons as they pass in front of the moon, and buckets of decorative Halloween paint that, artlessly hurled at the wall, nonetheless manages to yield perfect repeated silhouettes of witches and black cats. Betty also enlists a friendly cow to punch out jack-o'-lantern eyes, assembly line style, with its horns.

Oddly enough, none of the classic Hollywood horror movies of the 1930s had marketing campaigns tied to Halloween. Though widely celebrated, the holiday was not the focus of much commercial exploitation beyond party decorations and costume patterns during the Depression years. Universal Pictures premiered *Frankenstein* in Detroit at Thanksgiving 1931 – complete with newspaper ads framing the film's title with the problematic image of a turkey (not exactly the kind of imagery modern film marketers are likely to ever again embrace). Under new management, Universal would begin to aggressively market Halloween tie-ins for its franchised characters of Dracula, Frankenstein's monster, the Mummy, and the Wolf Man (along with many others) in the early 1960s. By 1999, with the explosive growth of DVD releases of its classic films, the studio spent a reported twenty million dollars to spread the message that "Universal IS Halloween."

Hollywood Halloween observances appeared during the Depression era in *As the Earth Turns* as well as in the Ken Maynard western *Smoking Guns* (both 1934). In 1937, Monogram's social drama *Boy of the Streets*, starring Jackie Cooper, paid a passing homage to Halloween, as did Fox's *Boy Friends* (1939), in which Jane Withers spends All Hallow's Eve in a nightclub. The short subject *Holiday Highlights* (1940) anticipated the ultra-commercialization of the holiday with a blackout gag depicting a witch pulling an advertising banner behind her broomstick (perhaps inspired by the previous year's unforgettable spectacle of Margaret Hamilton as a skywriting Wicked Witch of the West in MGM's *The Wizard of Oz*).

During the thirties, forties, and fifties, Hollywood studios routinely used Halloween as a venue for spooky publicity photos, usually unrelated to specific films, but which guaranteed certain stars wide press exposure during late October. At MGM, legendary glamour photographer George Hurrell posed more than one publicity still of Joan Crawford fashionably decked out as a witch. Other stars given the October 31 photo treatment at various studios included child performers Jackie Cooper and Shirley Temple, Betty Grable, Veronica Lake, and Jeanne Crain. Horror superstars Boris Karloff and Bela Lugosi do not seem to ever have been called into service by their studios for Halloween publicity, although they sometimes lampooned their screen personas at other holidays, including Easter and Christmas. One memorable still from the late 1930s shows Lugosi in his Dracula cape playing poker with Santa Claus. One giveth, the other taketh away.

Today, both Karloff and Lugosi are highly visible at Halloween, due to their descendants' ongoing efforts to commercially promote and license their images for a variety of merchandise, including masks, model kits, limited-edition bronzes and artwork, Halloween makeup, books, videos, coffee mugs, calendars . . . the list goes on. Halloween 1997 saw the long-awaited appearance of the classic horror actors on U.S. postal stamps, the result of aggressive petitioning by the estates. Sara Karloff, daughter of Boris, recalls that her father referred to Halloween simply as the "busy season" in his later years, after his old films were released to television and he himself was in high demand for entertainment/variety shows in late October.

"Now it's my busy season," says his daughter, who sometimes keeps up an appearance and interview schedule her father could never have dreamed of, even at the height of his studio fame. "The year of the stamp issuance, I did almost two hundred media interviews. One day I did twenty radio interviews back to back." She is frequently invited to high-profile, heavily attended conventions like Chiller Theatre, held every Halloween weekend in Rutherford,

New Jersey, and has gotten used to long lines of autograph seekers, eager for the seasonal chance to have a living Karloff to sign photos and memorabilia of Boris.

Another favorite Halloween destination for Sara Karloff most Octobers is the Witch's Dungeon Classic Movie Museum in Bristol, Connecticut. The museum's proprietor, Courtlandt Hull, is the great-nephew of Henry Hull, who played the Werewolf of London in Universal's 1935 film, as well as the great-nephew of Josephine Hull, who appeared on Broadway with Boris Karloff in *Arsenic and Old Lace*. Hull, a sculptor and restorer of vintage carousels, began his seasonal displays of classic movie monsters as a teenager in the 1960s, and the Witch's Dungeon remains one of a handful of Halloween attractions specifically devoted to Hollywood. One of the museum's perennial, life-size displays, of course, is Karloff in his most famous film, the 1931 *Frankenstein*.

As the only child of the man who immortalized the Frankenstein monster, Sara Karloff is always expected to get into the holiday spirit, but she doesn't have quite the same appreciation of the macabre that her father's fans have. At the Halloween theme park Spooky World, in Foxboro, Massachusetts, "I was prevailed upon – actually, I was strong-armed – into taking the haunted hayride. I ended up with my face in the hay, because I am a devoted wuss and I really don't like to be discomforted or scared. One year I was invited to Madison Scare Garden in New York, and I hung on to my husband so tightly that when I came out, I was as white as a sheet and soaking wet."

Has she ever been persuaded to make herself over as the Bride of Frankenstein for Halloween? "No, but I did once ask my husband if *he'd* ever consider being the Bride, and I could dress up as the monster. But I wasn't surprised that he said no," she laughs.

During World War II, Karloff *père* was still playing in the smash stage version of *Arsenic and Old Lace*. Unable to break his stage contract to appear in Frank Capra's 1944 film version, he was replaced by Raymond Massey, who played the on-the-lam killer whose features have been altered by a drunken plastic surgeon to resemble . . . Boris Karloff's. The film takes place on Halloween in Brooklyn. Cary Grant, as a just-married drama critic, pays a honeymoon's-eve courtesy call on his maiden aunts, only to discover that they are a pair of dotty but well-meaning serial killers who have recently put a succession of elderly men out of their presumed misery with carefully calibrated doses of arsenic, slipped into lovingly home-crafted elderberry wine. Although Halloween, per se, amounted more to window dressing than to a major theme, it was nonetheless the first time a feature motion picture presented a story completely framed by the holiday, and familiar Halloween icons adorned the picture's opening credits. Vincente Minnelli's *Meet Me in St. Louis*, released the same year, contained what many still believe to be the best evocation of an early-twentieth-century American Halloween ever filmed: a short but priceless sequence in which child star Margaret O'Brien is initiated into the holiday's ancient, ritual mysteries. The next year's screen adaptation of Betty Smith's best-selling novel *A Tree Grows in Brooklyn* omitted the book's memorable trick-or-treating episode, although it would be spectacularly restored as an impressionistic ballet in the 1953 Broadway musical version.

Walt Disney's animated 1949 adaptation of Washington Irving's story "The Legend of Sleepy Hollow" added Halloween to Irving's tale of the Headless Horseman, forgetting that the Dutch settlers of the Hudson River Valley in 1819 had no All Hallow's Eve tradition whatsoever. Irving's story did, however, employ an uncarved pumpkin as the Horseman's head; Disney anachronistically upgraded it to a jack-o'-lantern. (What Irving would have made of Bing Crosby as narrator-crooner is anybody's guess.) In 1952, Donald Duck's nephews starred in *Trick or Treat*, a short musical cartoon that was, arguably, one of the most important media influences on the postwar candy-begging tradition. It played in theaters for almost the entire month of October that year, and was later shown on television, providing an attractive Halloween behavior template for millions of baby boomers.

The late boomer generation was attending high school and college in 1978, when Irwin Yablans and Moustapha Akkad presciently changed the title of their forthcoming film *The Babysitter Murders* to *Halloween*. They had enlisted the young filmmaking team of John Carpenter and Debra Hill, who agreed to deliver the picture in less than a month for three hundred thousand dollars. Carpenter had previously directed *Assault on Precinct 13* (1976), which featured some striking subjective-camera work as well as an eerie score, which Carpenter himself had composed.

*Halloween* opens with a prologue in which a teenage girl, Judith Myers, has her boyfriend over for a Halloween-night bedroom tryst. The sequence is shot in a single, four-minute take, using the recently perfected Panaglide camera, which made smooth tracking shots possible without the use of dollies. The handheld camera affords the audience the subjective viewpoint of an unseen prowler, gliding like a jungle cat in and around the house. The camera takes us to the kitchen, where "we" quietly remove a butcher knife from a drawer. The boyfriend, who has quickly finished his business, leaves. Our unseen alter ego picks up a plastic clown mask and places it over the camera lens, and the scene continues framed by a pair of eyeholes. The camera sweeps up the stairs and enters the girl's bedroom. She sits seminude at a dressing table, brushing her hair. "Michael?" she asks, with surprised annoyance, and then again with abject horror as the knife plunges into her again and again. The killing completed, the camera scurries downstairs and out the front door to the sidewalk, where a pair of adults are arriving home. "Michael?" the man asks, and the camera angle becomes detached and objective. We see that our point of view has been a diminutive figure in a clown costume; the man removes the mask and we see a very young, blank-faced boy, still holding the bloody butcher knife in a frozen pose.

We learn that the boy is six-year-old Michael Myers, of Haddonfield, Illinois, who has killed his older sister for no apparent reason on Halloween 1963. He remains in a catatonic state for fifteen years, and becomes an obsession for his custodial psychiatrist, Dr. Sam Loomis (Donald Pleasence). Just before Halloween 1978, while being transferred to another facility, Myers escapes and returns to Haddonfield, where he begins stalking a baby-sitter named Laurie Strode (Jamie Lee Curtis). Wearing a mimelike mask, he begins savagely killing Laurie's sexually adventurous friends and, in the film's most harrowing scene, corners the girl in a louvered bedroom closet, the doors of which splinter like matchsticks as Laurie fends off the killer with a wire coat hanger. The psychiatrist arrives and shoots Michael repeatedly. He appears to fall dead but, as soon as no one is watching, mysteriously disappears.

Audiences did anything but disappear as *Halloween* rolled out in city after city in the fall of 1978. The major studios had declined to distribute or even view the film, and Irwin Yablans released *Halloween* himself, through Compass International Pictures, which he headed. He admitted that he was forced to "bring the picture in through the back door" and book engagements in less desirable "perimeter" theaters. Advertising expenses amounted to less than half of what major distributors were paying in these same venues. Favorable word of mouth quickly spread, and weekly grosses began to double. *Halloween* was on its way to becoming the highest-grossing independent film of all time, earning nearly fifty million dollars theatrically.[12]

---

12. *Halloween* has since relinquished its top-grossing status; the domestic revenue for *The Blair Witch Project* (1999) now exceeds $144 million, but considering that the average American movie ticket has nearly tripled in price since 1978, *Halloween* is still doing rather nicely.

A truly iconic film, *Halloween* has inspired endless critical commentary and analysis, but very little of it has explored *Halloween*'s relationship with its titular holiday. By the time *Halloween* appeared in theaters, almost completely baseless urban legends about the dangers of Halloween – poisoned candy, razor blades in apples, and so forth – were casually accepted as fact across America. A new tide of conservatism was taking hold, the cultural traumas of the Vietnam and Watergate eras having left a large portion of America cynical, or at least skeptical, about the promises of an inclusive, expansive democracy. Halloween, the one major holiday that was unofficial, and therefore uncontrolled, was a natural magnet for American anxieties about social disconnections. It was also a despiritualized holiday ripe for new myths and rituals. John Carpenter's *Halloween* would play a major role in the holiday's cultural reinvention.

Anthony Timpone is editor of *Fangoria*, a magazine consecrated to contemporary horror films like *Halloween*. There is probably no one in the world with a more authoritative knowledge of the screen careers of characters like Michael Myers. Myers, he notes, is the single most popular character his magazine covers, and readers keep a steady stream of *Halloween*-related article requests flowing, even during periods when the series is dormant. But Timpone can also vividly remember when Halloween had nothing to do with butcher knives or serial killers. Coming of age as a trick-or-treater in Queens, New York, in the late sixties and early seventies, he understood that "Halloween was pretty much all about candy. It wasn't a celebration of horror and darkness and spooks." Aside from plastic monster masks and perfunctory skeleton imagery – virtually no one any longer perceived the image of a skull in the traditional jack-o'-lantern – death itself now was pretty much off Halloween's radar screen, and any honest acknowledgment of the relevance of All Souls' Day to the holiday was essentially nonexistent. By the late 1970s, *Star Wars* costumes dominated the Halloween market.

Mortality and the uncanny – public-domain concepts, if there ever were, – had been supplanted by the lucrative, legally enforceable trademarks of entertainment conglomerates. And corporations, unlike individuals, do enjoy the prospect of eternal life, at least if they play their cards right.

*Halloween* was more than just the first film to fully exploit the holiday. In a stroke, it reconnected the celebration of October 31 to primal anxieties about life and its aftermath. In his book *The Movies on Your Mind*, the psychoanalyst Harvey R. Greenberg astutely observes that "from the cinema's earliest beginnings, the 'weird' genres – horror and much of science fiction – have administered a flamboyant, far more popular prescription for thanataphobia than the sobering insights of psychoanalysis." Cathartic death rituals, as represented by the horror movie, have always served a necessary psychological function. "By participating in the macabre pageant of weird cinema," Greenberg writes, "we tilt at the myriad deaths conjured up from childhood conflict and injury. We shriek and grin and mock at alien, yet familiar deaths, delighting for a few moments in our dubious victory over both our infantile distortions and the grim truth of mortality."

In *Halloween*, the dormant power of death is buried inside a little boy in the same way that the holiday's essential relationship to death had been repressed, transformed, and trivialized as children's fun and games. When Donald Pleasence tells the Haddonfield sheriff about watching Michael Myers grow up in a mental hospital, he is also making a comment on Halloween's primal power: "I watched him for fifteen years, sitting in a room staring at a wall, not seeing the wall, looking past the wall, looking at this night, inhumanly patient, *waiting* for some secret, silent alarm to trigger him off. Death has come to your little town, Sheriff. You can either ignore it or you can help me to stop it."

Director Carpenter's facility in eliciting cathartic scares can be traced, in part, to the fear rituals of his own childhood. "I'd go to the Southern Kentucky Fair and pay twenty-five cents to go into the Haunted House," he told *The New Yorker* in a 1980 profile. "You'd walk down a dark hallway, and when you stepped on a certain place it would make things jump out at you – it scared the hell out of me! Your expectation built up and up. I went again and again, to learn how it worked. *Halloween* was maybe a way of being young again and scared, and innocent in that way."

Carpenter's original music featured a relentless, minimalist title theme, echoing but not imitating Bernard Hermann's classic, stripped-down score for *Psycho*, a film also invoked by the casting of *Psycho* star Janet Leigh's daughter, Jamie Lee Curtis, in the lead. (The character of Sam Loomis also had his name lifted from *Psycho* – Sam Loomis was the name of Janet Leigh's lover, played by John Gavin.)

Although *Halloween* was widely lauded as a tour de force of directorial planning and control, one of its most memorable effects was almost improvisational. With virtually no budget for original makeup designs, Michael Myers's trademark white mask was actually a recycled and repainted mask of William Shatner on *Star Trek*, which hadn't sold well at Halloween, or anytime, according to its designer, Don Post. The utter blankness of the mask was matched by an equally deadpan physical performance by actor Nick Castle. "I would go up to John and say, 'How should I play this?' and he would say, 'Just walk.' The mask itself was doing more acting than I was."

Audiences projected their deepest fears onto the blank screen of Michael Myers's mask, and other filmmakers, sensing a trend, projected their own highest hopes. If imitation is indeed the sincerest form of flattery, then *Halloween* is one of the most excessively complimented films in history. The slasher genre may have had its formative roots in *Psycho*, but *Halloween* was the immediate inspiration for an avalanche of nubile-teenagers-stalked-by-a-maniac movies. Paramount, which turned down distribution rights to *Halloween*, quickly put a cinematic clone of its own into production. *Friday the Thirteenth* (1980) received almost uniformly terrible reviews, but was popular enough to spin off seven sequels revolving around a hulking, hockey-masked killer named Jason Voorhees. In *Nightmare Movies*, novelist and genre critic Kim Newman notes, "Usually, a significant date is referred to in the title, marking some past atrocity that will be replayed in the present." Beyond the *Friday the Thirteenth* films, these include *Mother's Day* and *Prom Night* (both 1980), *Graduation Day*, *Happy Birthday to Me*, *Hell Night*, and *My Bloody Valentine* (all 1981), *New Year's Evil* (1982), *Silent Night, Deadly Night* (1984), *Home, Sweet Home* (a 1985 Thanksgiving-themed carve-'em-up), and *April Fool's Day* (1986). Just as the celebration of Halloween traditionally involved an evolutionary give-and-take with other holidays, so too did *Halloween* inform the celebratory rituals of other slasher films. It might even be argued that the actual holiday depicted in many of these films is, in fact, Halloween in everything but name, involving as they do the ritual harvesting of human beings, the frequent display of masks, and the recurrent theme of the return of the dead.

*Halloween* had been rereleased theatrically for Halloween 1979, and the release of the first sequel, *Halloween II*, coincided with the original film's network television premiere in 1981. In the meantime, the first film's 1980 videocassette release had shattered all previous sales for a horror film.

Rather audaciously for a sequel, the film picks up exactly where *Halloween* ended, and does little tinkering with the original premise. John Carpenter and Debra Hill once more produced and wrote the script, and directorial duties were assigned to Rick Rosenthal, perhaps the only Harvard alumnus to ever direct a slasher film.

Rosenthal's psycho-thriller short subject, "The Toyer," had brought him to the attention of Carpenter's agent.

Following a replay of the first film's ending, Laurie Strode is rushed to Haddonfield Memorial Hospital for treatment of her stab wounds. The role is once more played by Jamie Lee Curtis, who had, by this time, become typecast as a horror ingénue – the previous year she had appeared in no fewer than three such films: John Carpenter's *The Fog* as well as *Prom Night* and *Terror Train*. Michael Myers isn't the only evil afoot in Haddonfield; the only other patient we see admitted is a little boy holding a bloody towel to his mouth, a razor blade embedded in his tongue. Clearly, Halloween in Haddonfield this year is a total bummer.

Fearing that Michael is not yet finished with his work, Laurie begs the hospital staff not to sedate her, to no avail. And, indeed, Michael is soon paying his respects, well outside of ordinary visiting hours. Dr. Loomis, meanwhile, uncovers evidence that Michael's killing spree is in honor of the Celtic festival of Samhain (which actor Pleasence badly mispronounces, as do other performers throughout the *Halloween* series) as well as a reason for Michael's obsessive interest in Laurie Strode: she is actually his younger sister, raised by another family after the awful events of Halloween 1963.

The original *Halloween* depicts four deaths, all rather discreetly by modern horror-movie standards. Far more graphic in its blood-letting, *Halloween II* piles up ten corpses before Dr. Loomis decides to ignite a tank of ether, incinerating both Michael and himself in the equivalent of a traditional sacrificial bonfire . . . or so it seems.

Rosenthal, with returning cinematographer Dean Cundey, effectively resurrected Carpenter's spare, wide-screen visual style, and Rosenthal added some atmosphere of his own. "What I tried to do was make a picture that had a little of the visual style of the German expressionists . . . contrasts, shafts of light, oblique angles . . ." One link to the early German cinema was the choice of Michael Riva, grandson of Marlene Dietrich, as production designer. But hints of creative conflicts appeared in the press. According to *Fangoria*'s Timpone, the grislier footage was added for commercial reasons without the nominal director's involvement. Rosenthal only noted, diplomatically, that *Halloween II* was "an interesting hybrid."

Interesting, perhaps, but often at the expense of credulity. As *Newsweek*'s David Ansen asked, "Why do the nurses never turn on the lights at this hospital? Why does Laurie appear to be the only patient in the whole joint? Why does the entrance door suddenly lock when she is trying to enter, when a minute before it was open? And where did the madman, who's been sitting motionless in a psycho ward for fifteen years, pick up his knowledge of Celtic mythology? Better not to ask." By beginning to hint at explanations and motives for its previously inscrutable bogeyman, the screenplay arguably undercut a major dramatic strength. No longer a mere psychopath, Michael Myers also seemed to be metamorphosing into a kind of supernatural October superhero, impervious to all manner of lethal force. Like a vampire, he represents death, but also the alluring possibility of surviving death. *Halloween II* ultimately did only about half the business of its predecessor, possibly because the intervening three years had seen so many *Halloween* imitators that the sequel no longer had quite the "event" cachet it might have exploited in a less crowded field.

There was, however, one audience member for whom *Halloween II* was especially unforgettable.

On December 7, 1982, an elderly couple in Fullerton, California, was brutally murdered. Francis Harmitz was stabbed twenty-four times; his wife, Aileen, nineteen times. On nothing more than a hunch offered by the Harmitzes' son, the police confronted the couple's handyman, thirty-one-year-old Richard

Delmer Boyer of El Monte, who had previously borrowed money from the victims. After an hour of intense questioning, during which Boyer's repeated requests for a lawyer were ignored, the police were about to release him, at which point Boyer suddenly shouted, "You're right. I can't live with it. I did it. I didn't mean to do it. But I did it."

As described in court documents, Boyer was a drug-soaked mess, a habitual user of alcohol, cocaine, marijuana, LSD, Quaaludes, amphetamines, and angel dust. On the day of the killings, he had ingested a pint of whiskey, taken speed, and possibly smoked pot. He also had injected cocaine that day with a friend, and attempted to sell a shotgun to his parents to repay his share of the drug buy. Unsuccessful, he asked his friend to drive him to the Harbitzes' neighborhood in Fullerton. He claimed that the couple greeted him cordially. But after he noticed a wallet on a dresser, he "started just freakin' out," and a headache he had been experiencing escalated into the sensation of "someone hitting him in the back of the head with a hard object." Finally, just before he started stabbing Mrs. Harbitz, he perceived a "foggy figure" which looked like a killer in a horror movie. Boyer thought the movie might have been *Halloween*, or possibly *Friday the Thirteenth*.

A first trial ended with a hung jury, and he was tried for a second time in 1984. Boyer offered an audacious defense: high on drugs and alcohol, he had experienced a harrowing cinematic "flashback" and could not distinguish reality from a remembered horror movie. Dr. Ronald Siegel, a psychopharmacologist called by the defense, identified the culpable movie as *Halloween II*, which included a scene of an elderly couple watching *Night of the Living Dead* on television while their house was invaded by Michael Myers, in search of a butcher knife. Boyer had originally watched *Halloween II* under the influence of angel dust, marijuana, and alcohol, the defense claimed, and spontaneous and involuntary flashbacks were a documented side effect of certain drugs, especially LSD, which Boyer had used since adolescence.

On May 23, 1984, *Halloween II* was shown to an Orange County jury, the first time in U.S. legal history that a commercial motion picture had been submitted as evidence at a murder trial.[13] In the end, however, the panel was not moved by Boyer's slasher-movie defense, and the presiding judge (who had the discretion to sentence Boyer to life in prison without the possibility of parole) sentenced the killer to death. Appeals ensued. In 1989, a retrial was ordered by the California Supreme Court on the grounds that Boyer had been improperly denied his Miranda rights. "We confront the relatively rare but distressing case in which the outcome is determined by the constable's blunders," the court opined. Boyer's tape-recorded confession was ruled inadmissible at the new trial, but physical evidence, including the defendant's knife and bloody slacks, were deemed admissible. The U.S. Supreme Court declined to hear an appeal, and Boyer was tried again in 1992. He was once more found guilty and sentenced to death. Ten years later, the man who achieved media notoriety as the "*Halloween II* killer" is still appealing his case, his ability to repeatedly escape death approaching that of the fictional Michael Myers.

Universal continued the franchise in 1982 with *Halloween III: Season of the Witch*, with a complete departure from the Michael Myers story line. Veteran actor Dan O'Herlihy plays Conal Cochran, a megalomaniacal toymaker intent on hatching the biggest Halloween prank of all time. Under the cover of Silver Shamrock

13. As far as this author has been able to determine, only one other "horror-movie defense" has ever been offered in a murder trial. In 1928, in London's Hyde Park, a Welsh carpenter named Robert Williams slashed his own throat as well as that of an Irish housemaid, Julia Mangan. Williams survived, and offered the unsuccessful explanation that he had been possessed by a vision of the actor Lon Chaney in his horrific "vampire" makeup for the 1927 film *London After Midnight* at the time of the crime.

Novelties, Cochran has somehow stolen a five-ton slab from Stonehenge ("the ancient, sacrificial circle") and transported it to his mask-making factory in Santa Mira, California[14] ("You wouldn't *believe* how we did it!" is all the explanation offered). In a mission-control-style laboratory, Cochran has tapped into the monolith's paleolithic powers. By combining particles of the slab with advanced microchip technology, he creates a line of Halloween masks that will unleash the forces of darkness when activated by a top-secret signal embedded in a prime-time Halloween broadcast. We have already seen what Cochran's masks can do: they cause insects and rattlesnakes to explode from your head. All across America, kids count down the days and hours to Silver Shamrock's "Big Giveaway" on Halloween night, already mind-controlled by the incessant jingle of a truly irritating television commercial. A well-meaning doctor who knows Cochran's secret attempts to derail the demented plot . . . but, then, what fun would that be?

*Halloween III* is less a horror movie than a sardonic satire on the corporate co-opting of Halloween itself, a trend, of course, partly set in motion by the megasuccess of Carpenter's original film. It also remains the only full-scale fictional interpretation of urban legends about Halloween booby traps and terrorism. But neither reviewers nor audiences responded favorably to the tongue-in-cheek approach. An attempt to merchandise replicas of the film's deadly masks – a witch, a skull, and a jack-o'-lantern – fell flat (they were simply too tired and generic), but is nonetheless historically important as an early attempt at the practice now universally known as product placement.

One lesson learned from *Halloween III* was very simple: the public liked Halloween to be scary, not satiric. As a result, Michael Myers was brought out of mothballs for *Halloween 4: The Return of Michael*

14. A jokey reference to the fictional town in the progenitor of all paranoid cinema, Don Siegel's *Invasion of the Body Snatchers* (1955).

*Myers* (1988), released on the tenth anniversary of the original film and referred to in publicity as a "triumphant rebirth" of the series. Universal had dropped the franchise after the disappointing performance of *Halloween III: Season of the Witch*, and the series returned to its independent production roots. Of the original cast members, only Donald Pleasence returned (and his presence as Dr. Loomis was considered so important to the film's fortune that he managed to negotiate above-the-title billing alongside executive producer Moustapha Akkad). The unavailability of Jamie Lee Curtis – who had finally broken out of her scream-queen straitjacket for mainstream success in projects like *A Fish Called Wanda* (1988) – necessitated some narrative radical surgery.

The last time we saw Laurie Strode, at the end of *Halloween II*, she seemed to have escaped the ether-tank holocaust that consumed both Dr. Loomis and Michael Myers. For practical reasons, however, in the sequel it was posited that Michael and Loomis had both survived, though badly burned, and that Laurie had gotten married, had a daughter (none-too-cutely named Jamie) and died with her husband in some unpleasant, undetailed accident.

Michael once more escapes from a mental hospital (a place, we are told, where "society dumps all its nightmares," though a far better case might be made for horror movies as a collective nightmare landfill) and makes a beeline for his niece, now adopted by another family. By this time in the series, Michael's function as a perverse Christ figure is quite evident; like a demented messiah, he spends purgative periods in wilderness exile (in this case, the loony bin), only to regularly reappear on the cusp of a pseudoreligious holiday in order to demonstrate his remarkable talent for self-resurrection. *Halloween 4* is the only film in the series to depict any figure of religious authority, and here it is a crackpot preacher, who nonetheless enunciates the eschatological underpinnings of the *Halloween* universe: "Apocalypse, the end of the world, Armageddon, it's always got a face and a name. You can't kill damnation, mister. It don't die like a man dies."

*Halloween 4* is graced by the superior performance of child actress Danielle Harris as Jamie, who effortlessly embodies Harvey Greenberg's observation that "the artless logic of the child's mind weaves death into the fabric of its perceptions or misperceptions of its world." Jamie is taunted by her classmates for not wearing a Halloween costume to school. "She doesn't have to," one of them jeers. "At Jamie's house, it's *always* Halloween. Her uncle's the bogeyman!" Putting on their Halloween masks, they razz her mercilessly for having dead parents and killer kin. Like a classic fairy tale (a genre famously obsessed with infanticide), the film itself takes the shape of a coming-of-age ritual, initiating protected childhood into the grown-up world of random violence and personal annihilation. The secular Loomis embodies the priestlike function once served by *Dracula*'s Professor Van Helsing and his crucifix, but psychiatry's authority proves fallible as the doctor tries to wrap his rational mind around the problem of unmitigated, undying evil. In the film's disturbing final scene, medicine is helpless as Jamie, possessed by Michael Myers, dons a festive clown costume and dispatches her stepmother with a butcher knife. "A feminist slasher is probably not what the pioneers of the women's movement had in mind," wrote *New York Times* critic Caryn James, anticipating the next sequel. "But at least she'll be different."

In *Halloween 5: The Revenge of Michael Myers* (1989), Jamie is under Dr. Loomis's care, and the last film's final murder seems not to have happened at all. The girl has, however, developed a full-fledged psychic link with her serial killer uncle, which allows director Dominique Othenin-Girard to flex new variations on the series' trademark subjective tracking shots. A tone of almost desperate religious hysteria underscores the film. Michael rises again, after a baptism in a fast-running creek. Jamie's dialogue during the

173

scream sequences consists almost exclusively of improvisations on "Oh, God, help me, God!" but God maintains a terrible silence. During the inevitable Michael Myers bloodbath that ensues (in which even teenagers who practice *safe* sex are butchered), Jamie finally cries out to Dr. Loomis, "Everybody's dead! I want to go home!" The good doctor gives her the bad news: "That's the *first* place he would look." "I prayed that he would burn in hell," says the doctor at one point, "but in my heart I knew that hell would not have him." In the end, Michael Myers doesn't even have to bother with the usual death/damnation/resurrection ritual. He simply disappears, and the audience understands full well that he will be back some October hence.

The sixth film eschewed a title numeral and was called simply *Halloween: The Curse of Michael Myers* (1995), and, by general consensus, is the nadir of the cycle. This time the death themes were not restricted to the screen — actor Donald Pleasance died of a heart attack during filming, which may help explain some bizarre lapses of continuity and a frequently incomprehensible plot line. A young woman, who, we eventually deduce, is the grown-up Jamie of the previous two installments, is impregnated by a satanic cult so that her baby can be the main course in a druidic blood sacrifice (the film topically reflects the mid-1990s hysteria over ritual satanic abuse). Jamie manages to save her newborn child, but she herself is gruesomely impaled by Michael Myers. Her baby is protected by Tommy Doyle (Paul Stephen Rudd), one of Jamie Lee Curtis's baby-sitting charges in the original film, who has spent his formative years discovering that Michael Myers bears an ancient Celtic curse that obligates him to kill family members to ensure the survival of the larger tribe. A Realtor relative of Laurie Strode (and therefore Michael's marked kin) moves his own family into the jinxed 1979 murder house that no one else will buy, and they all become instant targets for holiday homicide. When Michael is finally put down by Tommy Doyle, ordinary bludgeoning does the trick, which is a bit strange, because we've so often witnessed bullets bouncing right off him.

About halfway through the original *Halloween* cycle, critics began to complain loudly about the perceived misogyny of the *Halloween* series and its many imitators. A recurrent motif (far more prevalent in the imitators) was the swift and merciless punishment of teenage sex by gruesome death, with young women disproportionately dispatched. Oddly, conservative media commentators failed to see any useful connection with their own just-say-no-to-sex-and-drugs political agenda, but many Christian evangelical groups would eventually have field days staging moralistic Halloween "hell houses" graphically depicting the most extreme retributions for premarital sex, including AIDS and botched abortions.

Male critics were most vociferous in their knee-jerk condemnation of *Halloween*-inspired films, but women provided some of the most intelligent responses. Charlotte Low Allen, a commentator for National Public Radio, noted that films like *Halloween 4* were "end products of our society's efforts to ban or neutralize two powerful human phenomena: male aggression and religion." Unacknowledged or officially repressed, interest in these issues persists, "but in crude underground forms."

> We enlightened denizens of the late twentieth century are like Lady Macbeth, who scoffs, "Tis the eye of childhood that fears a painted evil." Horror movies play on our sneaking suspicion that the painted evil may be out there seeking the ruin of souls; that death, instead of pleasant annihilation, may be the beginning of eternal disquiet.

In *Men, Women and Chainsaws: Gender in the Modern Horror Film* (1992), Carol J. Clover offers a radical reassessment of the misogynist assumptions underlying slasher-film criticism. Rather than encouraging men to victimize women, she writes, movies like *Halloween* instead offer a complicated and multilayered medium in which viewers shift viewpoint allegiance between victim and victimizer: "Just as attacker and attacked are expressions of the same self in nightmares, so they are expressions of the same viewer in horror film. We are both Red Riding Hood *and* the Wolf; the force of the experience, in horror, comes from 'knowing' both sides of the story."

The ultimate point of audience identification, Clover argues, is "the last girl," emblematized by Jamie Lee Curtis in *Halloween*, who ultimately rises against her tormentor and emerges empowered and triumphant.

Slasher films, however, did not emerge triumphant from the 1980s, scuttled by their copycat profusion. "By the early 1990s, the bottom pretty much fell out on the horror-movie business," says *Fangoria* editor Timpone. "The only things going into production in '91, '92, and '93 were the big-budget gothic remakes like *Bram Stoker's Dracula* and *Mary Shelley's Frankenstein*, but you weren't seeing any of these low-budget horror movies. Some of them were going direct to video, but they were pretty much garbage. Basically, the genre was dead." Timpone traces the expansive growth of Halloween-season haunted houses to the demise of slasher pictures. "Fans of hard-core horror needed an outlet, so they started turning to spook houses. A lot of the people involved were young people who grew up with the slasher films and they decided to incorporate that stuff into their haunts because it was also cheap, the same way a lot of those slasher movies were cheap. All you needed was a guy with a chain saw in a mask, and he could chase patrons through the woods for a night. It was pretty easy to do those kind of entertainments. And the audiences who weren't getting their fill at the drive-in – or, more recently, at the multiplexes – could now see the stuff enacted live and in 3-D."

Michael Myers was often blurred in the public imagination with other celluloid serial killers, who, in obvious homage to the *Halloween* series, generally wore masks. In 1988, Mark Branch, an eighteen-year-old resident of Greenfield, Massachusetts, reportedly fixated on the Jason character from the *Friday the Thirteenth* movies (who wears a hockey mask), stabbed to death Sharon Gregory, a nineteen-year-old community-college student. Charged with the crime while still at large, Branch immediately became the focus of wildfire rumors that he would inevitably return to Greenfield on Halloween – presumably with butcher knife and Jason mask – to slaughter even more young people. An adult Halloween parade was cancelled, and trick-or-treating was restricted to daylight hours on the day preceding the holiday. Police also expressed fear that independent pranksters would don Jason costumes and risk violent retaliation from overreacting citizens. "The media has hyped the Jason angle so far that this community is sitting on pins and needles in fear," Greenfield police chief David McCarthy told the *Boston Globe*. "Youngsters are in fear that Jason is going to come back."

Branch did not return to Greenfield (he hanged himself before he could be apprehended), but three years later a similar panic overtook Massachusetts college campuses. Several variations of an urban-legend-style rumor circulated at least six New England schools. A psychic who had appeared on the Oprah Winfrey television show, it was said, foretold a 1991 movie-style Halloween campus massacre. (No such guest ever appeared on the show.) Some variations on the rumor attributed the prediction, quite inaccurately, to Nostradamus. Then it was rumored that many campuses had already decided to close on October 31. Frightened students at the University of Massachusetts demanded that their school be closed as well. Wheaton College spokesman Donald Stewart told the Associated Press that "as you debunk one rumor, the details seem to mutate into another, so we have to debunk them serially." He added "the kids who want to believe it will continue to talk about it. Some are enjoying the delicious, macabre element . . ."

"Delicious" and "macabre" are perfectively descriptive of Tim Burton's *The Nightmare Before Christmas* (1994), directed by Henry Selick, a tour de force of stop-motion animation in which Jack Skellington, the ectomorphic "Pumpkin King" of the village of Halloween, discovers the adjacent domain of Christmas and experiences a transformative, Scrooge-like epiphany. The film taps into the long-forgotten historical links between Yuletide and All Hallow's – both holidays are New Year's festivals, after all, one pagan and one Christian. The weird, abusive pranks Skellington ultimately inflicts upon Christmas celebrants strongly echo the Austrian tradition of Krampus night, still observed on December 5 in cities like Salzburg and Tyrol, where the usually benign Saint Nicholas summons terrifying monsters (elaborately costumed) to chastise difficult children, as well as hapless bystanders. (Krampus night is the only day of the year it's technically legal to beat someone up in Austria). The resulting anarchy is more mean-spirited than anything Tim Burton cooks up, yet both Krampus night and *The Nightmare Before Christmas* share a basic acknowledgement that all holidays have a dark side, rooted in the death/rebirth dynamic basic to seasonal festivals throughout human history.

*Nightmare* was produced by Disney but released through the studio's Touchstone division, to distance it from Disney's usual animated fare and family-friendly imprimatur. The edgy imagery and spidery, Edward Gorey-ish characters were a far cry from *Beauty and the Beast* or *Aladdin*, and the film was considered a gamble by studio executives. Studio chairman Jeffrey Katzenberg told an interviewer that "we know it's not for three-, four-, and five-year-olds." They rolled it out gingerly in a limited number of theaters in mid-October 1993.

Disney's eighteen-million-dollar investment garnered nearly

seventy-two million dollars in worldwide rentals, nothing like the cost-to-profit ratio of Carpenter's original *Halloween*, but very respectable nonetheless. It also demonstrated that Halloween as a subject could capture the attention of a much wider demographic than the audiences for slasher films, and its twin-holiday focus substantially lengthened its shelf time in theaters. J. Hoberman, in *The Village Voice*, called *The Nightmare Before Christmas* "inventive, witty, brilliantly designed, fantastically labor-intensive and detailed well past the point of obsession. One would have to go back half a century to Disney's *Pinocchio* to find a Hollywood animated feature with an imaginary world so fully peopled and densely populated." *Newsweek*'s Richard Corliss memorably compared Danny Elfman's score to "Kurt Weill settings for Dr. Seuss verses."

Young audiences also enjoyed such films as Wes Craven's wildly popular, postmodern semi-spoof on the slasher genre, *Scream* (1996), which included strategic clips from *Halloween* and introduced its own iconic variation on the psycho-killer-in-a-death-mask—which, strongly resembling Edvard Munch's *The Shriek*, became one of the most popular Halloween disguises ever commercially marketed. Its sales were amplified considerably by *Scream 2* (1997) and *Scream 3* (2000).

Another 1996 film, *Trick or Treat*, directed by Charles Martin Smith, lampooned the ritual demonization of heavy metal music by such groups as the Parents' Music Resource Center. Nerdy Eddie Weinbauer (Marc Price) worships a deceased, snake-blood-drinking shock-rocker named Sammi Curr (Tony Fields), whose final album, *Songs in the Key of Death*, contains backward-playing messages that instruct Eddie on ways to eliminate his school enemies permanently. The school's Halloween dance becomes an especially memorable event, in the apocalyptic style of *Carrie*. The worst right-wing fears about satanic rock lyrics and the evils of Halloween are made grotesquely, ridiculously literal.

When the prospect of obtaining the services of Jamie Lee Curtis for a twentieth-anniversary *Halloween* sequel became a real possibility rather than a pipe dream, the filmmakers gave little worry to the fact that her character had been killed off after the second film. Instead, they just pretended that all the other *Halloween* films never existed. All the previous story lines after *Halloween 2* were simply wiped clean. In *Halloween H20: Twenty Years Later* (1998), we learn that Laurie Strode is alive and well and living in California under an assumed name. Always a good student (as opposed to her sexually active and summarily disposable friends), she has become the headmistress of an exclusive private school. To avoid further run-ins with her homicidal brother, she has faked her own death and moved as far from Haddonfield as possible. But Halloween still comes around every year without fail, and with it, renewed anxiety. After a failed marriage, Laurie has become a closet alcoholic, clingingly overprotective of her teenage son, John (Josh Hartnett), a student at the school. John has grown up hearing about Michael Myers every year, and he's sick of it. So, when Michael actually turns up to settle a twenty-year score with his sister, at first it seems like Laurie is just wigging out again. *The New Yorker*'s Anthony Lane called *Halloween H20*, directed by Steve Miner, "the only serious *Halloween* movie since Carpenter's original," with Laurie "now as much of a head case as Michael himself . . . you can feel the thunder in the air when they meet face to face." Laurie reenacts the obligatory "last girl" scenario with a vengeance, and, when she finally turns Michael into the equivalent of the Headless Horseman with the help of a fire ax, it is not at all clear how the series can plausibly continue.

However, it would be a mistake to underestimate the *Halloween* filmmakers' ability to play prankishly with audience expectations. The latest installment, *Halloween: Homecoming* (2002) is still unreleased at the time of this writing, but has been the subject of intense

Internet gossip among series fans, with leaked synopses of various script drafts and preview screenings producing "spoiler" revelations of plot surprises involving the return of series icon Jamie Lee Curtis. Appropriately, the story itself involves a group of cyber-mavens who stage a Halloween night Web broadcast from inside the original murder house. (One of the many working titles for the film, happily discarded, was *Halloween: Michael Myers.com*.) Directed by *Halloween 2*'s Rick Rosenthal, the picture has reportedly undergone many revisions and reshoots, and been subjected to considerable research-based fine-tuning. Today, even independently produced films look nervously over their shoulders, as if in fear of a slashing specter.

In contrast, the stark simplicity and phenomenal impact of the original *Halloween* required no nervous market research, no second-guessing, just a single-minded commitment to a straightforward plan. Producer Irwin Yablans recalled that "It was a total contrivance . . . a manufactured article to meet a need. There had never been a film about Halloween before."

As one of the characters in the film observed, "You can't kill the bogeyman." But does anyone really want to? The track record suggests not. Filmmakers, filmgoers, and the ancient energies of Halloween itself all conspire to keep him relentlessly, inexorably, and − above all − mischievously alive.

# SEPTEMBER 11 AND OCTOBER 31

ESPITE A VAST landscape of tombstone-decorated front lawns, make-believe haunted houses, and the infinitely replicated image of the jack-o'-lantern's skeletal grin, Halloween in America has always had considerable difficulty dealing with the reality of death. Divorced from their religious roots, both pagan and Christian, ancient customs of honoring the departed were long ago transmogrified into consumption rituals for the living. Rubberized images of zombies, vampires, and other monsters recalled to life have replaced the heartfelt memories of real ancestors. As one of the young characters in Ray Bradbury's *The Halloween Tree* comments about October 31 as observed in small-town Illinois, "we've forgotten what it's all about. I mean the dead, up in our town, tonight, heck, they're forgotten. Nobody remembers. Nobody cares."

On September 11, 2001, the worlds of the living and the dead collided with a cataclysmic force that the United States mainland had never experienced or even imagined. The world watched, stunned, as its greatest metropolis became its greatest necropolis. Although Halloween was not foremost in anyone's mind at the time of the attacks, it was the American calendar's next significant day of public congregation, and an obvious potential target for terrorism. The following weeks forced an unprecedented cultural debate about the meaning and purpose of Halloween.

"Turning an inherently ghoulish holiday into an inoffensive celebration can be a matter of delicate compromise," reported the *Baltimore Sun*. "Most retail stores ordered their Halloween costumes and accessories last spring, long before anyone knew a fake hand with a bloody stump might not seem in the best of taste after a national tragedy that left thousands dead." The paper noted that the Spencer Gifts store chain had removed severed limbs from its window displays, though not from its stores.

In Riverside, California, plans for a Halloween haunted house in which demon firefighters would lead visitors into the flaming maw of hell were quickly scrapped. "It didn't take long to realize that what we were planning would be completely inappropriate," an amusement park manager told the *Los Angeles Times*. In Florida, Busch Gardens was forced to rethink its own Halloween advertising at the last minute, due to its prominent use of the tag word "terror." In Washington, D.C., the multimedia Fright House Extreme Scream Park was canceled entirely. Held annually at the D.C. Armory, the Fright House unfortunately included apocalyptic images of the destruction of the U.S. Capitol, the Pentagon, and the White House. The Alexandria, Virginia, Jaycees deleted all overtones of bioterrorism from the depiction of a mad scientist's laboratory, while the Naples, Florida, Jaycees chapter attracted national media attention with a haunted house featuring the crowd-pleasing capture and electrocution of Osama bin Laden. "Every year we have an execution," Jaycees chair Lisa Douglass told the media. "This year we wanted to execute someone everyone hates."

What everyone really hated was September 11's untimely wake-up call from the Grim Reaper. While nothing could really have mitigated the shock of sudden death on such a mass scale, the Halloween-related aftermath of September 11 did underscore the degree to which American consumer culture has displaced its memento mori to murder mysteries, horror movies, and Halloween, where death reigns triumphant but no one ever has to grieve.

Not all cultures hold death at such a controlled distance. In Mexico and throughout Latin America, Halloween finds an odd reflection in the *Días de los Muertos*, or Days of the Dead, directly corresponding to All Saints' Day and All Souls' Day, on November 1 and 2. The saints are very little in evidence, and the holidays are instead devoted to celebration of departed souls, who are believed to return to earth, however briefly, eager to share in the feasting and merrymaking. The sentiment is serious, but the mood is festive (the closest European parallel is the Irish wake, and the nearest American equivalent the Dixieland jazz funeral). The first day is dedicated to the *angelitos*, or dead children; the second to those who perished as adults. Gravesites are cleaned and decorated, as if for a birthday party. Children's graves are adorned with toys and balloons, adult graves with the departed's favorite foods and drinks. Marigolds are everywhere. Fireworks flare. During the daylight hours, cemeteries become the location for picnics and partying, often accompanied by mariachi bands; the nights are given over to candlelit vigils with a night-long tolling of bells to guide wandering souls back to their loved ones. In homes, elaborate shrines called *ofrendas* are erected to the memory of dead family members, employing many of the same decorations seen in cemeteries, and are often personalized with photographs and possessions of the person being honored.

Food is essential to the Days of the Dead, the most traditional offering being *pan de muerto*, a sweet bread often decorated with a skull-and-crossbones design. Skull-shaped candy is also popular, especially with the recipient's name inscribed with frosting. Comic skeleton effigies, or *calaveras*, fashioned from papier-mâché or wood parody all manner of human activity; *catrines* and *catrinas*, a beloved subcategory, are male and female dandies whose bone-draped finery ridicules human vanity and social striving in a cultural transplantation of the medieval *danse macabre*.

The Days of the Dead evolved in the New World in a way very similar to the process that created Halloween in Europe. Although there is no direct connection between the Celtic and pre-Hispanic cultures, both had powerful conceptions of an afterlife, as well as traditions of human sacrifice. Their late-year festivals of death and life were appropriated and transformed by the early Christian church as a tool for colonization and conversion in both Europe and the Americas. Perhaps because modern Halloween has migrated far from its roots, picking up diverse influences en route, it has lost the spiritual dimension that still attends the Days of the Dead, far more firmly grounded in geography and tradition.

Over the past few decades, due to expanded trade and the inevitable penetration of American television and advertising, Halloween has taken significant root in Mexico, overlapping with the Days of the Dead in a way that many Mexicans view with alarm, especially as black cats, witches, and jack-o'-lanterns have begun to appear in cemetery tributes. Novelist Homero Aridjis called Halloween "cultural pollution." He urged economically pressed Mexicans to "leave aside all those Anglo-Saxon witches and ghosts and keep their money to buy bread and flowers to honor their dead." Border cities like Tijuana felt the brunt of American influence, and even instituted drives to teach school children about traditional Mexican customs and divert their attention from *jaloquin* and *triqui-triqui*, both offered as examples of language pollution. Conversely, the Days of the Dead have also taken root in many Hispanic communities in the United States, especially in the border states — sometimes to the displeasure of certain conservative Anglo-Catholics, who find the celebration sacrilegious, bordering on spiritualism. In Mexico, the tradition is a cherished treasure of national identity, and the church doesn't complain.

However, it would be a mistake to think that the Days of the Dead lack a commercial dimension. From the simplest food vendors at the gates of cemeteries to package-tour agents, the event is a gold mine for Mexican localities with especially vivid celebrations, such as Janitzio Island on Lake Patzcuaro, where candle-bearing boats transport chanting mainland celebrants to a hauntingly beautiful burial ground.

Rather than something to be feared, death is enthusiastically embraced and fully acknowledged as a part of life. As Octavio Paz has noted, the typical Mexican soul "chases after it, mocks it, courts it, hugs it, sleeps with it; it is his favorite plaything and his most lasting love."

In America, Halloween candy isn't skull-shaped, but in 2001, it may as well have been. The wave of anthrax terrorism after the September 11 attacks reawakened the twenty-year-old panic that followed the deadly Tylenol tamperings of the 1980s, as well as the perennial anxieties (however ill founded) about poisoned Halloween treats. In mid-October, a sales clerk at a Hackensack, New Jersey, Costco discount store reported that a person who appeared "foreign" bought seven thousand dollars' worth of candy, and the clerk assumed the worst. The Federal Bureau of Investigation determined that the individual intended only to resell the bulk purchase to retailers. One Chicago detective noted, "What is candy if it isn't sugary and powdery?" – these also being attributes of weapons-grade anthrax. The National Confectioners Association and Chocolate Manufacturers Association issued a statement cautioning alarmed consumers that some powdery residues were perfectly normal in the production of chocolates and other sweets. Many parents were unimpressed. One mother, who decided to postpone her twin toddlers' first foray into trick-or-treating, told the San Francisco Chronicle, "I don't know whether I'm a fatalist or just being pessimistic, but if [terrorists] can put anthrax in a letter, they can sure put it in candy and I don't even want them to touch it." Another mother said she planned to switch any candy her daughter collected with a secret, safe supply of her own. Overall, one national poll showed that fully two thirds of parents with young children said they would still permit trick-or-treating for Halloween 2001, with the other third curtailing the activity in one way or another.

In the 1980s, post-Tylenol trick-or-treating had shifted significantly from darkened neighborhood streets to brightly lit shopping malls, for reasons of perceived safety. But in 2001, shopping malls themselves became objects of fear. Shopping generally plunged sharply in the weeks following September 11, as consumers instinctively avoided places of high public congregation and limited egress. By the beginning of October, an e-mail message was replicating exponentially through cyberspace, reporting a secondhand story about a young American woman who had been dating (or, in some versions, was married to) an Afghani man who disappeared shortly before the World Trade Center attack, leaving a message warning her to avoid flying on September 11 at all costs, and also to stay out of shopping malls on Halloween. The message varied from region to region, often customized with convincing local details, and had all the hallmarks of a classic urban legend. But terrorists had demonstrated their capacity for nightmarish pranks, and the e-mail created widespread concern. The FBI investigated, and on October 15 issued an official press release debunking the hoax. But other hoaxes would follow. A home owner in Collier, Florida, was arrested after sprinkling flour over a basket of Tootsie Rolls left out for trick-or-treaters as an ill-considered joke. Originally charged with making a hoax weapon of mass destruction, a second-degree felony, he was ultimately sentenced to two years probation with community service.

In his syndicated column, the Reverend Jesse Jackson called for the cancellation of Halloween. "The president says we need to get on with our lives, and he is right. No threat of terror should keep us from going to work, to shop, or to the movies." But Halloween, to Jackson, was a different matter. "Even in normal years, it is a holiday of risk. Every year, we read tragic stories of children who are bloodied by sick tricks," Jackson wrote, either ignorant of the opposite reality behind the urban legends, or just willing to scare people for their own good. "The prospect for mischief is too great – if not from fanatics abroad than from our own homegrown crazies." Jackson suggested that older teenagers donate blood to the Red Cross for Halloween, and that younger children engage in fund-raising for emergency shipments of food. "So carve a pumpkin, light a candle, have a cookout. Invite friends over for a hot dog. But don't put your gremlins on the street, keep them close at hand this Halloween."

*Newsweek* essayist Carolyn Jabs defended her own decision to allow her children to dress up in fantastic and frightening costumes. "The most damaging legacy of terrorism," she wrote, "is the fear that monsters lurk everywhere, disguised as neighbors and co-workers." While she still planned "to censor any costume that resembles a wounded person, I will let my kids impersonate the scariest inhuman monsters they can imagine. For one night, I'll indulge my children – and myself – in the fantasy that evil is obvious and monsters are easily recognized."

In the immediate wake of September 11, organizers of the Greenwich Village Halloween Parade, the largest public celebration of its type in the country, briefly considered cancellation. But parade artistic director Jeanne Fleming finally decided that cancellation would be tantamount to capitulation. According to the parade's official statement,

> The catastrophic events of September 11 left us all suspended
> in a state of remorse, anger and powerlessness. At the Village

Halloween Parade, we understood that we had to rethink our plans, to envision a way to address the tragedy and turn our collective energies toward the healing of New York. We looked for guidance, as the Parade has always done, across the span of world cultures, and found one mythical creature, who, since ancient times, has always endured destruction to rise again – the Phoenix.

The firebird, suggested by parade puppeteer Sophia Michahelles, proved an inspired choice. The legend was originally recorded by Herodotus in the fifth century B.C., and later by Ovid in his *Metamorphoses*, based on the Assyrian mythology of a winged creature believed to live for five hundred years, at the end of which it would prepare its own funeral pyre of scented woods and spices, self-immolate in a cloud of incense, and rise again from its own ashes. The Greek word *phoenix* means "red" and refers to the bird's fiery plumage. The life, death, and rebirth of the phoenix symbolize the endless rising and setting of the sun, and, by extension, human immortality; variations on the myth are found in Egyptian, Chinese, Indian, and Hebrew folklore. Christian iconography has also occasionally appropriated the phoenix as a symbol of Christ's resurrection. In perverse counterpoint, a barely concealed image of the vampire-as-phoenix appears in one of the early cover illustrations for Bram Stoker's *Dracula* (1897).

None of its mythic reincarnations, however, had ever been accompanied by two thousand uniformed police officers and a hazmat squad, as it was on Halloween 2001 in New York City. Leading the parade from a site just a few blocks north of the police barricades which still cordoned off lower Manhattan, the phoenix led the parade north, accompanied by a phalanx of police and a marching band playing "Swing Low, Sweet Chariot." In previous years, any view of the approaching parade on lower Sixth Avenue would have had the World Trade Center towers as the dominant background element. Now, before an empty hole in the sky, there was only the Phoenix, its undulating form and twenty-foot wing-span animated by a half-dozen bamboo rods manipulated by marching puppeteers.

"Despite the buzz that costume shops were selling a lot of Mayor Rudolph Giuliani masks and firefighter suits, there were few parade goers dressed as the mayor or firemen," reported National Public Radio correspondent John Kalish. There were, however, squadrons of Lady Liberties (many of indeterminate gender), Uncle Sams, and Betsy Rosses. A caged Osama bin Laden was pulled along the avenue by costumed authorities, and a chain-saw-wielding psycho killer sported a GET OSAMA message on his back. There were Elvis impersonators, bats on bicycles, a giant scorpion, and an equally imposing simian skeleton (representing an endangered monkey species), whose bony fingers drifted out ominously over spectators. One lone parader from New Jersey, who called himself "Captain Silly," wore outlandish eyeglasses, loudly striped boxer shorts, and bulbous clown shoes and carried a placard commanding LAUGH AT FEAR, which earned special applause and media attention.

Nonetheless, the crowds were thinner and the floats fewer than usual. As one longtime parade supporter told NPR, "The media is filling us full of all kinds of fears . . . what do you expect?"

Halloween finally passed without terrorist incident, and the holiday itself emerged transformed in small but significant ways. In a country-wide display of what *Time* magazine called "Red, White and Boo," untold numbers of Americans instinctively created their own patriotic variations of Day of the Dead displays, with images of the World Trade Center replacing the leering death masks of traditional jack-o'-lanterns, and front-yard skeletons waving the Stars and Stripes. Public *ofrendas* in Mexico were similarly decorated. UNICEF donated its annual trick-or-treat largesse to children in

Afghanistan. Never before had so much genuine human feeling and civic solidarity been expended on a holiday previously notorious for its antisocial aspects. As a Towson, Maryland, costume-store owner observed, "Sometimes Halloween brings out the worst in people. But not this year."

Perhaps only temporarily, Halloween 2001 reconnected the holiday to some of its forgotten spiritual roots, in which even the silliest costume carries the vestige of profound human rituals of self-transcendence, death, and rebirth. As the Greenwich Village parade's artistic director, Jeanne Fleming (by a mildly macabre coincidence, the daughter of a funeral director), told the *Los Angeles Times*, the essential spirit of Halloween was, ultimately, "dancing in the face of death. Halloween is about bringing you to that edge, and realizing what it is to be truly alive."

# NOTES

INTRODUCTION: THE CANDY MAN'S TALE

BECAUSE IT WAS RAINING Basic facts about the murder of Timothy O'Bryan and the trial, conviction, and execution of Ronald Clark O'Bryan are drawn from the reporting of the *Houston Post*, the *Houston Chronicle*, the *Dallas Morning News*, and the *New York Times* in 1974, 1975, and 1984, as well as the Web site of the Texas Department of Criminal Justice. Details and/or quotations unique to any consulted source are cited accordingly below.

ONE NIGHT IN THE YEAR Margaret Mead, "Halloween: Where Has All the Mischief Gone?" *Redbook*, October 1975, p. 31.

IN CONSIDERABLE DEBT Glenn Lewis, "Tim's Tragedy: A Crescendo of Debts Began It," *Houston Post*, March 30, 1984, p. 3A.

NIGHT AND DAY Ray Bradbury, *The Halloween Tree* (New York: Alfred A. Knopf, 1972), p. 123.

ELIXIRS OF DEATH Rachel Carson, *Silent Spring* (1962; reprint, New York: Fawcett World Library), p. 24.

THOSE HALLOWEEN GOODIES Judy Klemesrud, "Those Treats May Be Tricks," *New York Times*, October 28, 1970, p. 56.

PERMISSIVENESS IN TODAYS SOCIETY Ibid.

CHILDREN WHO GO TRICK-OR-TREATING Joel Best and Gerald T. Horiuchi, "The Razor Blade in the Apple: The Social Construction of Urban Legends," *Social Problems*, vol. 32, no. 5, June 1985, p. 491.

THERE IS NO JUSTIFICATION Ibid.

DETROIT FIVE-YEAR-OLD Ibid., p. 490.

SEASONAL DITTY Joel Benton, "Hallowe'en," reprinted in Ruth Edna Kelley, *The Book of Hallowe'en* (Boston: Lothrop, Lee & Shepard, 1919), pp. 176–177.

ATLANTA'S MAYOR AND CITY COUNCIL Nathaniel Sheppard, Jr., "Atlanta and Miami Curbing Halloween," *New York Times*, October 31, 1980, p. A14.

TRICK OR TERROR *New York Post*, October 29, 1982, p. 1.

FALSE SENSE OF SECURITY Suzanne Daley, "Fear of Tainted Candy Prompts Wide Concern for Halloweeners," *New York Times*, October 30, 1982, p. A16.

WE AS HUMAN BEINGS "Candy Man Dies After Losing Last Appeals," *Houston Post*, March 31, 1984, p. 1A.

## CHAPTER 1: THE HALLOWEEN MACHINE

AS THE FALLEN LEAVES R. Chambers, *The Book of Days* (London: W&R Chambers Ltd., 1864), vol. 2, p. 399.

GROTESQUE CLOUD-CUCKOO-LAND Jessica Mitford, *The American Way of Death Revisited* (New York: Alfred A. Knopf, 1998), pp. 14–15.

RECENT BOOK Martha Stewart, *Halloween: Delicious Tricks and Wicked Treats for Your Scariest Halloween Ever* (New York: Clarkson N. Potter, Publishers, 2001).

IT IS NOW THE MOTHERS Margaret Mead, "Halloween: Where Has All the Mischief Gone?" *Redbook*, October 1975, p. 34.

DEVOTED TO SUPERSTITIOUS RITES Charles Squire, *Celtic Myth and Legend* (1905; reprint, Van Nuys, California: Newcastle Publishing Co., Inc, 1975), p. 36.

ONE OF THEIR LEADING DOGMAS Ibid., pp. 37–38.

IT WAS CUSTOMARY Chambers, *Book of Days*, p. 538.

LORD JESUS CHRIST Charles J. Callan and John A. McHugh, *Blessed Be God: A Complete Catholic Prayer Book* (New York: J. P. Kennedy & Sons, 1925), p. 237.

SUMPTUOUS ENTERTAINMENT Chambers, *Book of Days*, p. 538.

LIGHTED UP WITH FLOWERS Ibid.

FOR WE ARE ALL POOR PEOPLE This traditional folk rhyme can be found in its entirety in Lesley Pratt Bannatyne, *Halloween: An American Holiday, An American History* (1990; reprint, Gretna, Louisiana: Pelican Publishing Company, 1998), p. 10.

IMPORTANT AND PORTENTOUS Chambers, *Book of Days*, pp. 549–550.

LIKE THE WORLD OF SATIRE Terry Castle, *Masquerade and Civilization* (Palo Alto, California: Stanford University Press, 1986), p. 6.

TWO HAZEL-NUTS Quoted in Ruth Edna Kelley, *The Book of Hallowe'en* (Boston: Lothrop, Lee & Shepard Co., 1919), p. 91.

THESE GLOWING NUTS Ibid., pp. 91–92.

GREAT FUN GOES ON Chambers, *Book of Days*, p. 520.

ANY MAIDEN MAY FIND William S. Walsh, *Curiosities of Popular Customs* (1897; reprint, Philadelphia and London, J. B. Lippincott Company, 1925), p. xii.

I THOUGHT I WAS DRAGGED Ibid., pp. 521–522.

SEVERAL WELL-AUTHENTICATED INSTANCES Ibid., p. 521.

ASHES WERE RAKED SMOOTH Kelley, *Book of Hallowe'en*, pp. 56–57.

AN HERB CALLED LIVELONG Ibid., p. 53.

SCOTTISH CHILDREN REPLENISHED Walsh, *Curiosities*, p. 510.

TOO PURITANICAL Jean Markale, *The Pagan Mysteries of Halloween* (Rochester, Vermont: Inner Traditions International, 2001), p. 112.

THE IRISH HAD PRECIOUS LITTLE Bannatyne, *Halloween*, p. x.

MISCHIEVOUS BOYS PUSH THE PITH Walsh, *Curiosities*, pp. 509–510.

IN THE UNITED STATES Ibid., p. 511.

THE EARLIEST DECORATIONS Stuart Schneider, *Halloween in America: A Collector's Guide with Prices* (Atglen, Pennsylvania: Schiffer Publishing Company, 1995), p. 13.

UNRELIABLE, CRAZY Donald Bogle, *Coons, Toms, Mulattoes, Mammies and Bucks: An Interpretive History of Blacks in American Films* (New York: Viking Press, 1974), p. 7.

HALLOWE'EN FAILURE The poem is also reprinted in its entirety in Kelley, *Book of Hallowe'en*, pp. 174–175.

WASHINGTON JEFFERSON JACKSON LINCOLN The complete skit appears in Elizabeth F. Guptill, *The Complete Hallowe'en Book* (Lebanon, Ohio: March Brothers, Publishers, 1915), pp. 75–84.

CARNIVALESQUE HARVEST COSTUMES Sheila Young, "Betty Bonnet's Halloween Party," *Ladies' Home Journal*, October 1917, p. 38.

STRETCH FOR SOPHISTICATION Claire Wallis, "Pyramids of Fun for Halloween," *Ladies' Home Journal*, October 1924, p. 117.

ABOUT TEN THOUSAND DENNISON DEALERS Dan and Pauline Campanelli, *Halloween Collectables* [sic]: *A Price Guide* (Gas City, Indiana: L-W Books, 1995), p. 107.

STOP HALLOWEEN PRANKSTERS The packaging is reproduced in Schneider, *Halloween in America*, p. 177.

THE STREET WAS JAMMED Betty Smith, *A Tree Grows in Brooklyn* (1943; reprint, New York: HarperPerennial, 1992), pp. 170–171.

HIGH-SPIRITED EXTENSION Diana Karter Appelbaum, *Thanksgiving: An American Holiday, An American History* (New York and Bicester, England: Facts on File Publications, 1984), p. 186.

VARIEGATED AND BEWILDERING ATTIRE "Young America in the Streets," *New York Times*, November 25, 1881, p. 8. Quoted in Appelbaum, *Thanksgiving*, p. 188.

VARIED AS THE WHIMS OF A COQUETTE, "Fun of a Lively Sort," *New York Times*, November 27, 1885, p. 8. Quoted in Appelbaum, *Thanksgiving*, p. 189.

YESTERDAY'S ANNUAL PERFORMANCE "City Urchins Revive Their Holiday Mask," *New York Times*, November 30, 1928, p. 8.

TIME WAS "Thanksgiving Mummery Strikes a New Low; Ragamuffins Find This Is a Depression Year," *New York Times*, November 25, 1932, p. 4.

PRANKS OF MASKED CHILDREN "Street Fights Mark Halloween in Harlem; 400 Parading Children Battle with Stones," *New York Times*, November 1, 1934, p. 3.

FOURTEEN YEAR-OLD BOY "Halloween Vandals Kill Connecticut Boy," *New York Times*, November 2, 1934, p. 3.

BEFORE HE DIED "Says Houdini Sent Word from the Beyond," *New York Times*, November 23, 1926, p. 15.

AUNT BESS COULD NEVER PASS Kenneth Silverman, *Houdini!!! The Career of Erich Weiss* (New York: HarperCollins, 1996), p. 428.

DECLARED TO THE PRESS "Abandons Hope of Communicating with Husband in Spirit World," *New York Times*, March 19, 1930, p. 21.

ROSABELLE ANSWER "Great Silence," *Time*, November 9, 1936, p. 48.

TINSELTOWN WAS ALREADY "Pixies Ride Again Tonight," *Los Angeles Examiner*, October 31, 1936, p. 1.

I DO NOT BELIEVE The Amazing Randi and Bert Randolph Sugar, *Houdini: His Life and Art* (New York: Grosset & Dunlap, 1976), p. 156.

IF THE DECORATIONS ARE SPOOKY ENOUGH Doris Hudson Moss, "A Victim of the Window-Soaping Brigade?" *American Home*, November 1939, p. 48.

HALLOWEEN AFFORDS Undated *Houston Chronicle* editorial, quoted in the *New York Times*, October 27, 1935, section 4, p. 8.

LETTING THE AIR OUT OF TIRES "Hits Halloween Revels," *New York Times*, October 23, 1942, p. 16.

A REHEARSAL FOR CONSUMERSHIP Gregory Stone, "Halloween and the Mass Child," *Social Problems*, vol. 13, no. 3 (1959), p. 379.

WAS THE CHOICE PROFFERED Ibid., pp. 374–375.

THERE WAS THE IDEA OF BEING Rochelle Santopaolo, interviewed by the author, August 2001.

NATIONAL CONFECTIONERS ASSOCIATION Angela Paik, "Halloween Has Grown Up: Adults Move In on the Fun," *Washington Post*, October 26, 2000, p. M3.

## CHAPTER 2: THE WITCH'S TEAT

ESTIMATED $30.3 MILLION Figures provided to the author by the tourist agency Destination Salem, January 2002.

OLD CANDLELIT HOUSES Advertisement in *Salem Haunted Happenings 2001 Official Guide* (tourist handout), p. 15.

REVENUE FOR TODAY Craig Wilson, "History Clashes with Commercialism," *USA Today* (online edition), October 24, 1997.

LONG-HELD HATREDS Arthur Miller, *The Crucible* (1954; reprint, New York: Bantam Books, 1959), pp. 5–6.

THEIR HUMAN URGES Frances Hill, *A Delusion of Satan* (1995; reprint, New York: Da Capo Press, 1997), p. 23.

UNGUENT WHICH . . . THEY MAKE Montague Summers, ed., *The Malleus Maleficarum of Heinrich Kramer and James Sprenger* (1928; reprint, New York: Dover Publications, 1971), p. 75.

WHEN THE WITCHES Candace Savage, *Witch: The Wild Ride from Wicked to Wicca* (Vancouver, British Columbia: Greystone Press, 2000), p. 5.

BIOGRAPHICAL CHARACTERISTICS John Putnam Demos, in *Entertaining Satan: Witchcraft and the Culture of New England* (Oxford and New York: Oxford University Press, 1982). See chapter 3, "Witches: A Collective Portrait," pp. 57–94.

POST-TRIAL TRACTS An excellent selection of historical writings on the Salem hysteria can be found in Frances Hill's anthology *The Salem Witch Trials Reader* (Cambridge, Massachusetts: Da Capo Press, 2000).

LO, THERE YE STAND Nathaniel Hawthorne, "Young Goodman Brown," *The Complete Novels and Selected Tales of Nathaniel Howthorne* (New York: The Modern Library, 1937), p. 1041.

POWERFUL AS A TELESCOPE L. Frank Baum, *The Wonderful Wizard of Oz* (1900; reprint, New York: Dover Publications, Inc., 1960), p. 141.

WITCH CREAM A reproduction of this 1895 illustration, perhaps the earliest example of the witch image in advertising, can be found in Savage, *Witch*, p. 9.

MOST FUNDAMENTALISTS DO NOT BELIEVE Margot Adler, *Drawing Down the Moon: Witches, Druids, Goddess Worshippers and Other Pagans in America Today* (Revised edition; New York: Beacon Press, 1989), p. viii.

IF TRUTH IS THE FIRST CASUALTY John Koch, "Kitsch Boils Over in Witty Look at Salem," *Boston Globe*, April 20, 1999; online transcript.

AVAILABLE ON VIDEO *Witch City* is distributed by Picture Business Productions, 200 Park Avenue South, Suite 1612, New York, NY 10003.

INVESTIGATION RAPIDLY SPIRALED Elizabeth Loftus and Katherine Ketcham, *The Myth of Repressed Memory* (New York: St. Martin's Press, 1996), p. 228.

REFUTING THE EXISTENCE Daniel Goleman, "Proof Lacking for Ritual Abuse by Satanists," *New York Times*, October 31, 1994, p. A13.

SACRIFICES ARE NECESSARY Jack T. Chick, "The Trick" (Chino, California: Chick Publications, Inc., 1989), unpaginated pamphlet.

POLITICALLY-ACTIVE AND PROFITABLE CULT Jay Rogers, "Child

Sacrifice in the New Age: Salem's Witch Cult and America's Abortion Industry," online article at forerunner.com.

RAISED MORE THAN TEN THOUSAND DOLLARS G. Jeffrey MacDonald, "Not All in Salem Welcome Witches," *Detroit Free Press* (online edition), October 27, 2000.

TIRED OF TACKY TOURIST TRAPS? *Salem Haunted Happenings 2001 Official Guide*, p. 20.

## CHAPTER 3: HOME IS WHERE THE HEARSE IS

COSTS AROUND FIVE HUNDRED THOUSAND DOLLARS Rich Correll, interviewed by author, October 2001.

THE WITCH IS DEAD, AND THIS IS HER HEAD Ray Bradbury, "The October Game," *The Stories of Ray Bradbury* (New York: Alfred A. Knopf, 1980), pp. 791–792.

THE GOLD STANDARD FOR HAUNTED HOUSES Jeff Baham, "The Secrets of Walt Disney World's Haunted Mansion," *Haunted Attraction* no. 22 (2000), p. 22.

I WAS VERY SHY IN SCHOOL Bob Burns, interviewed by author, November 2001.

FOUNDER OF THE GLOBAL HALLOWEEN ALLIANCE Rochelle Santopaolo, interviewed by author, June 2001.

DES PLAINES, ILLINOIS, HOME OWNERS Courtenay Edelhart, "Feud Sends Horror Display to Its Grave," *Chicago Tribune*, October 29, 1995, section 4, p. 5.

YOU DON'T GENERALLY SEE SPOOK HOUSES Cameron Jamie, interviewed by author, April 2002.

IT WOULD BE A PROVOCATIVE CONCEPT Leonard Pickel, interviewed by author, December 2001.

URINARY INCONTINENCE For this, and a wealth of other anecdotes related to the Haunted Mansion, see Jeff Baham's unofficial Web site tribute at doombuggies.com.

HORROR HOTEL MONSTER MUSEUM David Lady, interviewed by author, June 2001.

LONG-DISTANCE LOVE AFFAIR WITH HALLOWEEN Clive Barker, interviewed by author, October 2001.


## CHAPTER 4: THE DEVIL ON CASTRO STREET

ONE NIGHT A YEAR Randy Shilts, *The Mayor of Castro Street: The Life and Times of Harvey Milk* (New York: St. Martin's Press, 1982), p. 54.

TWELVE POLICE OFFICERS Michael R. Gorman, *The Empress Is a Man: Stories from the Life of José Sarria* (Binghamton, New York: Harrington Park Press, 1998), p. 218.

UNLIKE MOST PARADES Jack Kugelmass, "Wishes Come True: Designing the Greenwich Village Halloween Parade," in Jack Santino, ed., *Halloween and Other Festivals of Death and Life* (Knoxville, Kentucky: University of Kentucky Press, 1994), p. 212.

NO ORGANIZED EVENT "Uncle Donald's Castro Street," unsigned historical commentary at the Web site www.backdoor.com.

IT'S A ONCE IN A YEAR CHANCE Tim Vollmer, "Halloween San Francisco Style," *San Francisco Sentinel*, October 25, 1990, p. 37.

TEAR-GAS CANISTERS Susan Stryker and Jim Van Buskirk, *Gay by the Bay: A History of Queer Culture in the San Francisco Bay Area* (San Francisco: Chronicle Books, 1996), p. 77.

JUST FIFTEEN YEARS AGO Shilts, *Mayor of Castro Street*, p. 249.

SUDDEN INFLUX Diana Christensen, "CUAV Column," *Bay Area Reporter*, November 5, 1984 (typescript). Gay, Lesbian, Bisexual and Transgender Historical Society of Northern California (GLBTHS) research collection, San Francisco.

DRESS AS BASEBALL PLAYERS Diana Christensen, "Avoiding Violence on Halloween," *Bay Area Reporter*, October 25, 1984. Unpaginated clipping. GLBTHS collection.

STICKING ME INTO VIETNAM Christensen, "CUAV Column."

IN ITS EARLY YEARS Andrew Jacobs, "The Parade: Too, Too? Or Too Much?" *New York Times*, October 29, 1995, Section 8, p. 6.

FOR FIVE YEARS CUAV Open letter, October 18, 1986. GLBTHS collection.

ONUS OF CONFRONTING Ibid.

WE ENCOURAGE PEOPLE Undated 1986 CUAV press release. GLBTHS collection.

GAWK AT THE QUEERS Kathleen Baca, " 'Queers' Take Back Halloween," *San Francisco Sentinel*, October 25, 1990, p. 4.

EASIER TO GET A CONDOM Chip Johnson, "The Devil, You Say? San Francisco Faces Halloween Exorcism," *Wall Street Journal*, October 30, 1990, p. 1.

AMID FERVENT PRAYING Don Lattin and David Tuller, "6,500 Christians Attend S.F. 'Exorcism,' " *San Francisco Chronicle*, November 1, 1990, p. A2.

POLICE IN RIOT HELMETS Craig Marine and Jane Ganahl, "Prayer Army and 'Pagans' Tangle," *San Francisco Examiner*, November 1, 1990, p. A1.

STAYED AWAY FROM THEIR OWN NEIGHBORHOOD Jill Tregor, CUAV program coordinator, memorandum to board of directors, August 20, 1991. GLBTHS collection.

REPORTED FIFTEEN THOUSAND DOLLARS All fund-raising figures are taken from the 1993 Halloween flyer distributed by the Sisters of Perpetual Indulgence, Inc. GLBTHS collection.

A GRAVEYARD OF PREACHERS AND CHURCHES Dan Levy, "Evangelist Returns to S.F. for Halloween Prayers," *San Francisco Chronicle*, October 30, 1991, p. A15.

YOUNG WOMAN WRITHES ON A GURNEY Jeff McLaughlin, "Haunted

House Abortion Scene Sparks Protests," *Boston Globe*, October 30, 1991, p. 1.

WE HAVE SEVERAL DENOMINATIONS Virginia Culver, "'Hell House' Opens Its Doors," *Denver Post*, October 21, 1995, p. A1.

CATERING TO THE LOWEST LEVELS Virginia Culver, "'Hell House' Ignites Debate," *Denver Post*, October 21, 1995, p. B1.

280-PAGE MANUAL Gayle White, "Trick or Treat? No, Turn or Burn," *Atlanta Journal-Constitution*, October 19, 1997, p. H5.

I THINK THE DEPICTION OF HELL Celia Sibley, "Church's House of Scare," *Atlanta Constitution*, November 1, 1995, p. 3:1.

NO CUTE BABY-FACED DEVILS White, "Trick or Treat?"

A MADMAN IN THE PULPIT Michael Hirsley, "Churches Undaunted about Being 'Haunted,'" *Chicago Tribune*, October 31, 1993, section 2C, p. 1.

TERROR AND WONDER OF THE SPIRITUAL WORLD Ibid.

BLONDE 'NICOLE' WIGS Michael Granberry and David Ferrell, "O.J. Simpson Masks a Macabre Halloween Sensation," *Los Angeles Times*, October 8, 1994, p. A24.

NECK PROSTHESES Nancy Ryan, "Halloween Conjures Simpson Costumes," *Chicago Tribune*, October 23, 1994, section 2, p. 3.

SOME CONSUMERS Ibid.

BLOODY EFFIGY OF THE THROAT-SLASHED NICOLE Kenneth Fagan, "It's Morbid, It's Tasteless – It's Halloween," *San Francisco Chronicle*, October 29, 1994, p. A1.

THIS ISN'T EVEN THE SICKEST COSTUME Ryan, "Simpson Costumes."

REVISITATION OF THE RICHARD NIXON DISGUISE Fagan, "It's Morbid, It's Tasteless."

IDEAL CLIVE BARKER COSTUME Clive Barker, interviewed by author, September 2001.

AMALGAM OF SEXUAL EXCESS Clive Barker, introduction to *The Books of Blood*; text file provided by Barker.

SENT PARENTS A LETTER Kristina Marlowe and Andrew Gottesman,

"For Politically Correct, Halloween Can Be Frightening," *Chicago Tribune*, September 30, 1994, p. 1.

STALK OF BROCCOLI Ibid.

TEACHING ABOUT HALLOWEEN John Wildermuth, "Los Altos Schools Ban Halloween Activities," *San Francisco Chronicle*, October 12, 1995, p. A17.

MY KIDS ARE REALLY UPSET Ibid.

THE WITCH WHO SWITCHED John Wildermuth, "Halloween in Los Altos? Schools Say Yes," *San Francisco Chronicle*, October 18, 1995, p. A17.

EACH YEAR AS HALLOWEEN DRAWS NEAR "Countertrends," *Consumer Trends Reports*, May 2001, p. 6.

PART OF MY HERITAGE Marlowe and Gottesman, "Politically Correct."

PERFECT FOR A WHEELCHAIR "Halloween Costumes," October 16, 1997, backandneck.miningco.com.

SEVERAL UNIVERSITIES Clarence Page, "Blackface Students Need Better Schooling," *Chicago Tribune* (online edition), November 18, 2001.

GIANT VAGINA Buck Wolf, "Prize-Winning Genitalia," abcnews.com, November 2, 2001.

REAL EVIL CAN BE FOUND Kristine Holmgren, "Parent-Centered Jitters Haunt the Magic of Halloween," *Chicago Tribune*, October 31, 1996, p. 27.

CHARACTER ARMOR OF EVIL Lena Williams, "For More Youths, It's Always Halloween," *New York Times*, October 25, 1989, p. C1.

TEENAGERS ARE OFTEN REBELLIOUS Ibid.

DEAR [MERCHANT] Hands Off Halloween Campaign model letter, reprinted at American Academy of Pediatrics Web site (www.aap.org).

ADULTS HAVE CELEBRATED HALLOWEEN "Brewers Are Asked to Put Skeletons Back in Closet," *Los Angeles Times*, October 26, 1994, p. D2.

MYSTERIOUS CAT DISAPPEARANCES Wayne Knabb, "Halloween Is Bad Luck for Area's Black Cats," *New Orleans Times-Picayune*, October 27, 1990 (unpaginated clipping).

MANY COUPLES ARE WAITING LONGER "Pets," *Consumer Trends Report*, May 2001, p. 6.

ERNEST PECEK Associated Press, "Man Dressed as Vampire Dies after Stabbing Self Accidentally," November 1, 1981. Cited by Norine Dresser in *American Vampires* (New York: W.W. Norton & Company, 1989), p. 41.

MILTON TYREE Ray Richard, " 'Hunchback' Hanging Gag Ends in Death of Prankster," *Boston Globe*, November 2, 1988, p. 29.

MOWED DOWN BY SEMIAUTOMATIC GUNFIRE Edmund Newton and Vicki Torres, "3 Boys Returning from Halloween Party Slain," *Los Angeles Times*, November 2, 1993, p. 1.

STANDING AT THE ALTAR OF A CHURCH Ibid.

NORTHERN IRELAND TERRORISTS Shawn Pogatchnik, "The Terror Is Only Make-Believe in Northern Ireland This Halloween," *Chicago Tribune*, October 31, 1994, section 1, p. 3.

BUENA PARK, CALIFORNIA, GRANDFATHER Mike Downey, "A Real-Life Horror Story for Halloween," *Los Angeles Times*, October 22, 1999, p. A3.

ANTHONY DWAIN LEE Sarah Tippet, "Preparing for Court Show-down," Reuters report posted at abcnews.com, December 11, 2000.

QUITE A FEW OF THE FIRES "Devil's Night: The Flames Signal a Frightening Lawlessness" (editorial), *Detroit Free Press*, November 3, 1983, p. 10A.

URGED A LAW-AND-ORDER APPROACH "Signal Fire: Devil's Night Should Open Eyes to the Need for More Police" (editorial), *Detroit Free Press*, November 2, 1984, p. 10A.

TELEVISION CREWS . . . "FIRE BUFFS" Bill McGraw, "Keeping the Watch," *Detroit Free Press*, October 31, 1985, p. 11A.

RESURGENCE OF HALLOWEEN ARSON Statistical table accompanying Jodi S. Cohen, "30,000 Angels Quiet Devils," *Detroit News* (online edition), October 31, 2001.

ABANDONED AUTOWORKERS' HOUSING Amy Worden, "Halloween Tricks No Treat for Some Cities," apbnews.com, October 29, 1999.

CELEBRATION OF O-BON Mary Ganz, "Japan Stores Lead the Charge for Halloween," *San Francisco Chronicle*, October 30, 1988, p. A12.

AN AWKWARD ENCOUNTER Associated Press, " 'Little Monsters' Invade France in Confusing, Scary American Threat," *Chicago Tribune*, "Evening Update," October 30, 1995, p. 2.

DARKER AND MORE MACABRE FANTASIES John-Thor Dahlburg, "The Frost Is on the *Citrouille* as French Adopt Halloween," *Los Angeles Times*, October 31, 1997, p. A12.

## CHAPTER 5: HALLOWEEN ON SCREEN

NOW ITS MY BUSY SEASON Sara Karloff Sparkman, interviewed by author, September 2001.

MAJOR STUDIOS HAD DECLINED Avery Mason, "Yablans' 'Halloween' May Be Biggest Indie," *Boxoffice*, April 9, 1979. Unpaginated clipping.

SINGLE MOST POPULAR CHARACTER Anthony Timpone, interviewed by author, November 2001.

PRESCRIPTION FOR THANATAPHOBIA Harvey R. Greenberg, M.D., *The Movies on Your Mind: Film Classics on the Couch, from Fellini to Frankenstein* (New York: Saturday Review Press/E. P. Dutton and Company, 1975), pp. 197–198.

SOUTHERN KENTUCKY FAIR J. Stevenson, "Profile," *The New Yorker*, January 28, 1980, p. 47.

HOW SHOULD I PLAY THIS? Marc Shapiro, "The Shapes of Wrath," *Fangoria*, November 1989, p. 30.

USUALLY, A SIGNIFICANT DATE Kim Newman, *Nightmare Movies: A Critical Guide to Contemporary Horror Films* (New York: Harmony Books, 1988), p. 145.

VISUAL STYLE OF THE GERMAN EXPRESSIONISTS Peter J. Boyer, "Harvard Man Takes a Plunge in Crimson with 'Halloween' Sequel," *Los Angeles Times*, October 28, 1981.

INTERESTING HYBRID Ibid.

NURSES NEVER TURN ON THE LIGHTS David Ansen, "Eyeball to Eyeball," *Newsweek*, November 16, 1982, p. 117.

SUDDENLY SHOUTED, "YOU'RE RIGHT . . ." David G. Savage, "High Court Orders Retrial in Couple's Murders," *Los Angeles Times*, November 28, 1989.

COURT DOCUMENTS *People v. Boyer*, 48 Cal. 3d 247 (1989).

A RETRIAL WAS ORDERED David G. Savage, "High Court Orders Retrial in Couple's Murder," *Los Angeles Times*, November 28, 1989 (unpaginated clipping).

REPLICAS OF THE FILM'S DEADLY MASKS Aljean Harmetz, "*Halloween III* Masks to Help Scare Up Sales," *New York Times*, October 16, 1982 (unpaginated clipping).

ARTLESS LOGIC Greenberg, *Movies on Your Mind*, p. 197.

FEMINIST SLASHER Caryn James, "A Slasher Goes Back to Work," *New York Times*, October 22, 1988 (unpaginated clipping).

END PRODUCTS OF OUR SOCIETY'S EFFORTS Charlotte Low Allen, "Frightening Messages from the Movies," *Los Angeles Times Calendar*, November 13, 1998, p. 3.

JUST AS ATTACKER AND ATTACKED Carol J. Clover, *Men, Women and Chainsaws: Gender in the Modern Horror Film* (Princeton, New Jersey: Princeton University Press, 1992), p. 12.

BY THE EARLY 1990s Timpone interview.

FIXATED ON THE JASON CHARACTER Tom Coakley, "After Slaying, Fears Disrupt Halloween in Greenfield," *Boston Globe*, October 29, 1988, p. 21.

MEDIA HAS HYPED THE JASON ANGLE Ibid.

AS YOU DEBUNK ONE RUMOR Associated Press, "Rumors of Slayings on Halloween Sweep Campuses in New England," *New York Times*, October 30, 1991, p. A-18.

NOT FOR THREE-, FOUR- AND FIVE-YEAR-OLDS Betsey Sharkey, "Tim Burton's 'Nightmare' Comes True," *New York Times*, October 10, 1993 (unpaginated clipping).

THE ONLY SERIOUS *HALLOWEEN* MOVIE Anthony Lane, "Trick and Treat," *The New Yorker*, August 10, 1998, p. 79.

TOTAL CONTRIVANCE Frank Barron, " 'Halloween' Seen as Perennial Holiday Fare by Irwin Yablans," *Hollywood Reporter*, November 10, 1979 (unpaginated clipping).


# AFTERWORD: SEPTEMBER 11 AND DECEMBER 31

WE'VE FORGOTTEN WHAT IT'S ALL ABOUT Bradbury, *The Halloween Tree*, p. 118.

A MATTER OF DELICATE COMPROMISE Elizabeth Large, "Less Fright, More Fun," *Baltimore Sun* (online edition), October 28, 2001.

DEMON FIREFIGHTERS Abigail Goldman, Jessica Garrison, and Mitchell Landsberg, "A Lighter Version of Halloween," *Los Angeles Times*, October 23, 2001, p. A-1.

FRIGHT HOUSE EXTREME SCREAM PARK Large, "Less Fright, More Fun."

DESTRUCTION OF THE U.S. CAPITOL Christine A. Samuels and Rosalind S. Helderman, "A More Caring Scaring: This Year's Real-Life Fears Trump Made-Up Ones for Many," *Washington Post*, October 24, 2001, p. B-1.

OVERTONES OF BIOTERRORISM Ibid.

EVERY YEAR WE HAVE AN EXECUTION Associated Press, untitled online report, October 28, 2001.

CULTURAL POLLUTION Julia Preston, "The Day of the Ghouls vs. the

Day of the Dead," *New York Times*, November 2, 1996 (unpaginated clipping).

BORDER CITIES LIKE TIJUANA Sebastian Rotella, "In Tijuana, Traditional Day of the Dead Dawns Anew," *Los Angeles Times*, November 3, 1993, p. A-3.

WHAT IS CANDY Rudy Bush and Stanley Ziemba, "Cops Aren't Expecting an Unusual Halloween," *Chicago Tribune* (online edition), October 29, 2001.

NATIONAL CONFECTIONERS ASSOCIATION Ibid.

A PERSON WHO APPEARED FOREIGN Ronald Smothers, "F.B.I. Finds Bulk Candy Purchase to Be Harmless," *New York Times*, October 23, 2001, p. B-10.

I DON'T KNOW WHETHER I'M A FATALIST Anastasia Hendrix, "Halloween Fears: Concerns about Terrorism Prompt Wary Parents to Restrict Trick-or-Treating while Some Malls Nix Annual Parties," *San Francisco Chronicle* (online edition), October 29, 2001.

HOME OWNER IN COLLIER, FLORIDA Chris W. Colby, "North Naples Man Pleads No Contest in Halloween Anthrax Prank," *Naples Daily News* (online edition), March 14, 2002.

THE PRESIDENT SAYS Reverend Jesse L. Jackson, Sr., "No Masks This Year," *Chicago Tribune* (online edition), October 21, 2001.

THE MOST DAMAGING LEGACY OF TERRORISM Carolyn Jabs, "A Day for My Kids to Be Scary, Not Scared," *Newsweek*, October 29, 2001, p. 14.

THE CATASTROPHIC EVENTS OF SEPTEMBER 11 "This Year's Theme Is: Phoenix," undated announcement for 2001 Village Halloween Parade at parade Web site, www.halloween-nyc.com.

VAMPIRE-AS-PHOENIX For an illustration of the 1916 Rider edition of *Dracula*, see David J. Skal, *Hollywood Gothic: The Tangled Web of Dracula from Novel to Stage to Screen* (New York: W.W. Norton & Company, 1990), p. 37.

DESPITE THE BUZZ John Kalish, "Halloween in New York City," National Public Radio *Morning Edition*, November 1, 2001, author's transcript of broadcast.

SOMETIMES HALLOWEEN BRINGS OUT THE WORST Large, "Less Fright, More Fun."

DANCING IN THE FACE OF DEATH Dennis Arp, "To Haunt and Heal, It Takes the Village," *Los Angeles Times*, October 31, 2001, p. E-2.

# ACKNOWLEDGMENTS

Thanks are in order to numerous individuals for their support and assistance during the research and writing and publication of *Death Makes a Holiday*. At Bloomsbury USA, I am gratefully indebted to Karen Rinaldi, Colin Dickerman, Lara Carrigan (for her especially perceptive line editing and many editorial suggestions), Susan Burns, Andrea Lynch, Alona Fryman, and Sandee Yuen. Thanks especially to High Design for their striking cover design and interior illustration treatments, and to copy editor Greg Villepique. I am most grateful to my literary agents, Malaga Baldi of the Malaga Baldi Literary Agency and Christopher Schelling of Ralph Vicinanza, Ltd., and to my lecture agent, Scott Wolfman, for ongoing advice and professional encouragement.

Among those who most generously contributed their time, expertise, and enthusiasm to the project are Clive Barker, Bob Burns, Rich Correll, Cameron Jamie, David and Laura Lady, Leonard Pickel, Bob Quinn, Rochelle Santopoalo, Sara Karloff Sparkman, Anthony Timpone, and Taylor White. Others who provided suggestions, referrals, or simply answers to peculiar questions include Jay Blotcher, Ron Borst, Norine Dresser, Hilary Hinzmann, Bob Madison, Scott MacQueen, William G. Obbagy, and Laura Ross.

Research facilities included the Library of Congress; the Los

Angeles Public Library; the Margaret Herrick Library of the Academy of Motion Pictures Arts and Sciences (special thanks to Stacey Behlmer); the University of California, Los Angeles; the University of California, Berkeley; the San Francisco Public Library; the Glendale Public Library; and the Gay, Lesbian, Bisexual and Transgender Historical Society of Northern California (special thanks to Kim Klausner). In Washington, D.C., Elias Savada provided valuable microfilm research assistance. Archival photo research was conducted with knowledgeable care by I. Donald Bowden of AP/Wide World Photos, and Howard Mandelbaum, Ron Mandelbaum, and Buddy Weiss of Photofest.

A final, essential thank-you goes to my closest friend and life partner, Robert Postawko, who bravely endured a year-long invasion of our home by Halloween. I promise it won't happen again (at least until the next book).

# INDEX

# INDEX

# INDEX

# INDEX

New England
  witches in, 69, 73
  *See also* Salem, Massachusetts
*New Year's Evil* (film), 166
New York City
  Eden Musée in, 85, 86
  "fantasticals" parade in, 45–46
  Great Depression in, 46–47, 48
  homosexuals in, 125–26, 132, 189–91,
    192
  Madison Scare Garden in, 159
  ragamuffins in, 44–46
  Thanksgiving in, 45–47
*New York Post*, 14–15
*New York Times*, 5–7, 15, 46, 50, 77–78,
  132, 146, 173
*The New Yorker*, 165, 181
Newman, Kim, 166
*Newsweek*, 180, 189
*Night of the Living Dead* (film), 169
*The Nightmare Before Christmas* (film), 57,
  178–79
Nixon, Richard, 140–41
Northern Ireland, 150
*Nosferatu* (film), 155
Nostradamus, 177
Novak, Kim, 71
November 1, 21–22, 23, 185
November 2, 22, 185
November Eve, 17, 22
nudity, 119, 129
nuts, 26–27

O-Bon celebration, 152
Oak Park, Illinois, 139
O'Brien, Margaret, 160
O'Bryan, Ronald Clark, 1–3, 7–8, 10–13,
  15–16, 89
"The October Game" (Bradbury), 86
O'Herlihy, Dan, 170–71
Olympia, Washington, satanic ritual in, 77
"On Nuts Burning, Allhallows Eve"
  (Graydon), 26–27
open houses, Halloween, 52–53
Oprah Winfrey (TV show), 177
Othenin-Girard, Dominique, 173
Ouija boards, 40
Owens, David, 139

pagans, 72–73
paintings, witches in, 68
parades
  Death as grand marshal of, 18

and homosexuals, 125–26, 132, 189–91, 192
and "return of the dead," 18
and roots of Halloween, 18, 24
in Salem, 62
*See also specific parade*
Paramount Studios, 166
Parker, Whitney, 10, 11
Parris family, 63–64
parties, hosting Halloween, 86
Paul, Ru, 129
Paz, Octavio, 187
Peabody Essex Museum (Salem,
  Massachusetts), 60, 76
Pecek, Ernest, 149
Perrault, Charles, 68
Pez candy dispenser, 140
*The Phantom of the Opera* (film), 155
Philadelphia, Pennsylvania, Jaycee haunted
  house in, 103
Phoenix, 190–91
photography, 98–99
Pickel, Leonard, 100–108
pixies, 33
Playboy Mansion, 83–84
Pleasence, Donald, 167, 172, 174
poisoning. *See* tampering
Polanski, Roman, 72
political correctness, 142–45, 175
Pomona (goddess), 21–22
Post, Don, 110–11, 165
postcards, 36, 37–38, 40, 71
pranks. *See* trick or treat; tricks
Price, Marc, 180
*Prom Night* (film), 166, 167
*Psycho* (film), 165
public schools, Halloween in, 142–43
publicity photos, spooky, 157–58
pumpkins, 19–20, 35, 36, 38, 150. *See also*
  jack-o-lanterns
*Punch* magazine, 84
Puritans, 36, 59, 62–66, 68. *See also* Salem,
  Massachusetts
Putnam family, 65

Queer Nation, 135
Quinn, Bob, 74, 76

Rackham, Arthur, 70
ragamuffins, 46–47, 48, 52, 56
"recovered memory" movement, 77
Red Cross blood drive, 117, 189
religion, 72–74, 76, 80, 81–82, 172–73. *See
  also* fundamentalism, religious

# INDEX

# INDEX

# A NOTE ON THE AUTHOR

David J. Skal is the author of *Hollywood
Gothic*, *The Monster Show*, *V Is for Vampire*,
*Screams of Reason*, and, with Elias Savada,
*Dark Carnival: The Secret World of Tod
Browning*. With Nina Auerbach, he is co-
editor of the Norton Critical Edition of
Bram Stoker's *Dracula*. A longtime New
Yorker, he now lives in Los Angeles.

## A NOTE ON THE TYPE

The text of this book is set in Bembo. This type was first used in 1495 by the Venetian printer Aldus Manutius for Cardinal Bembo's *De Aetna*, and was cut for Manutius by Francesco Griffo. It was one of the types used by Claude Garamond (1480–1561) as a model for his Romain de L'Université, and so it was the forerunner of what became standard European type for the following two centuries. Its modern form follows the original types and was designed for Monotype in 1929.